PASTA

OTHER BOOKS BY KATIE & GIANCARLO CALDESI:

RECIPE NOTES

Unless otherwise stated: all fruit and vegetables are medium-sized; all fruit and herbs are fresh; all eggs are free-range and medium-sized.

All olive oil used in this book is extra-virgin olive oil.

Raw or lightly cooked eggs should be avoided by pregnant women, the elderly and very young children.

Recipes that contain nuts should be avoided by those with a known allergic reaction to nuts and nut derivatives.

Oven temperature: these are given for fan ovens. If you are using a conventional oven, increase the heat by around 20°C (you can also check with the manufacturer's handbook).

Photography
By Helen Cathcart

THE LONG & THE SHORT OF

PASTA

A Collection of Treasured Italian Dishes

Katie & Giancarlo Caldesi

hardie grant books

CONTENTS

THE LONG & THE SHORT OF PASTA

Pasta is a feeling as well as a fuel. In our opinion there is nothing quite so satisfying to eat as a bowl of hot pasta clinging to a rich, intense sauce – from the aroma of the sauce warming in the pan, the look of a dish that will surely quash your hunger to the first bite into al dente pasta that slides easily from fork to mouth.

No one can say for sure where pasta appeared first in the world. In its basic form it is a mixture of flour and water and as such could have been thought of by many people.

Although Marco Polo may have seen noodles on his visits to China it was already in Italy before he came back. At Cerveteri near Rome, we have seen Etruscan tomb paintings which show a bowl with flour and water, a rolling pin and even a cutting wheel dating to the 4th century BC. The Ancient Roman writer Apicius described making lagana, a forerunner to lasagne made from cooked sheets of flour and water. The famous 'ndunderi – a type of gnocchi made from flour and cheese – from Minori are from an ancient, possibly Roman recipe and have even been recognized by Unesco as one of the first types pasta.

In 1154 AD an Arab geographer, Al-Idrisi, wrote of strands of pasta made in Sicily, it was a technique introduced by the Arabs from Palestine. The lengths of pasta were dried and exported in huge quantities from Norman Sicily. There are documents dating from 1371 that reveal that the prices of macaroni and lasagne in Palermo were triple those of bread. As such it was a food enjoyed mostly by the aristocracy and the Jewish population.

Pasta was originally eaten with hands but the addition of sauces led to the widespread use of the table fork. In Medieval Italy ravioli was a popular dish often containing herbs and spices, mixed with cheese and eggs, then cooked in broth and finished with more spice and sometimes sugar. Lasagne too, would be coated with sugar and spice. Couscous, which are tiny beads of pasta was also brought to Sicily by the Arabs and is still made along the west coast of the island.

Lunch is the time in Tuscany to eat pasta. In most households you will find pots of ragù or tomato sauce in the fridge for such a time. We sometimes have a ball of leftover pasta dough in the fridge, so all I need to do is quickly roll it through the pasta machine and drop the strands into boiling water for a couple of minutes to make a quick lunch. However, dried pasta is perfectly

ACCORDING TO A STUDY OF GLOBAL FOOD TRENDS... PASTA IS THE WORLD'S FAVOURITE FOOD

acceptable and its quick cooking time makes it ideal for a meal when you have little time for preparation. Many Italians also eat it in the evening, or late into the night. Giancarlo remembers preparing *un spaghettata* in the early hours of the morning after a night of dancing: he would cook pasta and serve it with a little chilli, splashes of new olive oil, a handful of chopped parsley and some of the local sheep's cheese.

The nutrition

According to a study of global food trends by Oxfam pasta is the world's favourite food and a group of pasta producers has now proclaimed 25th October as World Pasta Day. Celebrations take place all over the world to recognise this combination of protein and carbohydrate that is both filling and inexpensive. With the addition of a sauce containing protein such as a ragù or fat such as olive oil, pasta will sustain you for a good few hours.

Pasta is relatively low on the GI scale amongst other carbohydrates, the glycaemic index shows the effect that carbohydrates have on our blood sugar levels. Cooking it al dente means that the release of sugar into the blood will happen more slowly than it would with overcooked pasta. And if you cool the pasta after cooking it and then either reheat it or eat it cold it will be even lower as some of it will become resistant starch that cannot be digested by our bodies so you will absorb fewer calories. Resistant starch is also good for our guts as it feeds the good bacteria.

By making your own sauces you can avoid the sugar-laden commercial alternatives and fussy-eaters will often tuck into carrots, onions and celery disguised in tomato sauces or ragù without realising they are eating vegetables. It is however worth remembering that in Italy pasta is served in small portions as a starter and never in huge bowls as we have become used to in the rest of the world.

What to eat if you don't or can't eat pasta?

Giancarlo was hit with a double whammy when his doctor told him some years ago he not only had Type 2 diabetes but was also gluten-intolerant. Pasta is a treat for him now and has to be gluten-free. After much experimentation we found the recipe on page 35 works brilliantly for stuffed or ribbons of pasta. To avoid the spike of glucose in his blood from carbohydrate we have been really happy to discover vegetable 'pasta' as an alternative.

Just because Mamma would never have had her ragù with anything but freshly made ribbons of pasta doesn't mean that her son couldn't enjoy his ragù (on page 99) with similar looking ribbons of steamed cabbage tossed in black pepper and butter. He is very happy to eat his favourite Caldesi sauce on page 58 on roasted courgettes, onions and aubergines and topped with a scattering of Parmesan and basil leaves. Courgetti, the spiralised lengths of courgette, are wonderful if very briefly sautéed with garlic, chilli and olive oil before being topped with the Roman sauce Alla Checca on page 46.

Difference between dried and fresh pasta

Italians don't judge fresh or dried as 'better' – they are just different. Generally fresh pasta is made with egg and flour and dried pasta is made with water and flour but there are some anomalies such as pici on page 33 or dried egg pasta usually sold in cardboard cartons to protect its fragile form.

All pasta in Giancarlo's household was fresh until the 1950s when dried pasta came onto the market and his mum was no longer tied to the kitchen table making it every day. I am sure she loved her new found freedom and time saving packets of spaghetti. However she and many other Italians never lost their love of freshly made pasta. Southern regions such as Sicily eat less fresh pasta than their northern counterparts and when it is made in the south it frequently contains semola flour and no egg in contrast to the rich egg pasta from the north.

For weekday meals we buy dried linguine, spaghetti and penne and sometimes splash out on the boxes of dried tagliatelle or fettucine egg pasta that cook in 4 minutes. Otherwise we make our own fresh stuffed pasta and ribbons when we have a little more time.

Shapes and sizes

There is a size and shape for particular sauces; peas or halved cherry tomatoes slip inside *paccheri*, the wide short tubes made in Campania and ragù made with finely chopped meat gets trapped inside *penne*. Tiny florets of broccoli and crumbled sausage meat sit snugly in *orrecchiete*, little ear shapes. Ragù alla Bolognese is never served on top of spaghetti, only tossed into fresh egg *tagliatelle* made so thin you are supposed to see the bells of the local church through it. Over the border in Tuscany wide ribbons of *pappardelle* are robust and opaque and are dressed with game or duck ragù. *Stelline* or little stars and *ditalini*, little fingers, go into soups. The combinations preferred by Italians are endless and each family, town and region has their favourites.

PASTA MADE WITH BRONZE DIES HELPS THE SAUCE STICK, GIVING A BETTER RESULT

Dried pasta

Originally pasta ribbons were hung over wooden poles outdoors and dried in the sunshine and light breezes of southern Italy. Dried pasta these days is made in factories and the lengths are extruded through metal dyes which gives it a smooth, slippery finish. This means it is less absorbent than fresh pasta and is ideally suited to wetter sauces made with wine and cooking juices such as seafood or the Romanesco sauce on page 139. If you can find pasta extruded through bronze dyes (it will often say *trafilata al bronzo* on the packet) it has a slightly rougher surface than a pasta made with a Teflon dye. The slight roughness mimics pasta made by a traditional wooden rolling pin which helps the sauce stick to the shapes and gives a better result to the dish. The ideal flour for dried pasta is pura semola di grano duro (pure durum wheat semolina).

We always choose an Italian brand of pasta such as Barilla or De Cecco. The maccheronari, or original pasta-makers from Campania, realised that Gragnano, further inland from the Amalfi Coast, had a particularly favourable, slightly humid climate which was perfect for slowly drying pasta. Today many Italians will only buy pasta from Gragnano as it is still such good quality. Others choose pasta from Abruzzo as they swear the water used to make the pasta gives it the edge.

COOKING & SERVING PASTA

 Pasta should be cooked in the biggest pot you have. It can then move around in the water without sticking together. Make sure the water is bubbling hard when you put in the pasta. It should always be cooked in plenty of well-salted water. It should be as salty as the sea so about 320 g (11¼ oz) pasta to 4 litres (7 pints) of water and 20 g (¾ oz) salt.

 Don't add oil to the water; it's expensive and rises to the surface rather than coating the pasta.

 Just before you've reached the cooking time on the packet, take out a strand of pasta and test it. If it is just tender, but still has some resistance, then it is ready – 'al dente', literally 'to the tooth'.

 Don't rinse the pasta after cooking. It will wash the last of the starch from the pasta that helps the sauce to stick to it.

 Always transfer the al dente pasta to the warm sauce. The best way to collect the pasta is with a 'spider' (a cobweb-shaped sieve) or a pair of tongs. As you transfer the pasta a few splashes of cooking water are added to the sauce, which helps to lengthen and flavour it.

 The pasta should finish cooking for a minute or two in the sauce to really absorb the flavour. Toss the pan or use tongs to move the pasta in the sauce to combine them both. Some of the starch from the pasta will release into the sauce and help thicken it. If the sauce becomes too thick, add a little of the pasta cooking water. The exception to this rule are raw sauces such as pesto, which are simply stirred through hot pasta in a bowl.

 Don't serve salad with pasta, particularly if it is dressed, as it will interfere with the flavour of the dish; eat it before or after the pasta course.

HOW TO USE...

SALT

Salt is an essential part of the Italian kitchen. Without it your food will never taste authentic. An average Italian pinch of salt is approximately 3 g (½ teaspoon), which is probably more than most non-Italians add. We have measured the salt quantities in some of the recipes when you cannot add salt to taste, for example to a ragù, before it is cooked. When you can, do keep tasting your food before serving it. This might sound obvious, but you would be amazed by the number of people who don't, and the end result can be disappointingly bland after all your efforts.

Adding salt can often make food taste sweeter. For example, adding the right amount of salt to a tomato sauce brings out the natural sweetness of the tomato, avoiding the need to add sugar.

If you were a little over generous with the salt, add a peeled small potato to the pot and it will absorb the salt. A squeeze of lemon juice helps, too.

CHILLIES

Having written cookbooks for years I have now realised it is pointless to state how much fresh chilli to put into a recipe. Long red or green chillies vary so much in heat you cannot tell by looking at them. Therefore, I encourage students in our cookery classes to taste the chilli. The heat is not in the seeds but in the pith, so you need to taste the chilli from around the middle, not at either end where there may be no pith. Only by tasting it will you know how much to add to your dish.

HERBS

For appearance and aroma pasta is often finished with herbs. It makes all the difference if freshly chopped parsley or a few leaves of basil are added to the serving bowl. However don't be tempted to add thyme leaves or rosemary needles to a dish. Better to rest a whole sprig on top that can be easily removed.

CHEESE

You can always spot the non-Italian if they order cheese with the seafood pasta, it is just not approved of by most Italians as it disguises delicate flavours. There are some exceptions – we found the diners in Amalfi enjoying Parmesan on their fish pasta. What we would suggest is encourage your guests to taste the food first before adding Parmesan.

PEPPER

We always use freshly-ground black pepper to dishes as it gives a kick of heat and spice and we like the look of it. There are some Italians that refuse to touch it or only use white pepper on fish or delicate flavours, the choice is yours.

OLIVE OIL

Always use extra-virgin if using oil at all – don't expect to use rapeseed or sunflower to give the same results. Extra-virgin olive oil is extremely good for you; we cook with it and use it to dress cold foods. Its smoke point is only just lower than other oils on the market and the taste, in our opinion, can't be beaten. We never deep fat fry in it as it would be too expensive and it just can't take the heat. Swirl olive oil onto hot pasta particularly if the dish looks dry. Italians use it to garnish hot food such as soups or pasta, the heat makes the aromatics in the oil fill the air with the most appetising and appealing scents. Often oil is the dressing – so don't stint on it.

BREAD WITH PASTA

Where there is a table of food in Italy, there is bread. No Italian ever eats a meal without bread. It is unthinkable to leave your pasta bowl or plate with sauce still clinging to it – much better to mop it all up with a hunk of bread. They even have a word for it – *la scarpetta* is the piece of bread used for such a purpose. In the Catholic religion bread represents the body of Christ and as such is treated with respect. I have seen people kissing bread before throwing it away or admonishing children for playing with it. Bread even has its own special day in the calendar: on 13th June it is the celebration of Sant'Antonio da Padova and it is traditional to bring bread to the local church to be blessed.

HOW TO MAKE FRESH PASTA

HOW TO MAKE FRESH PASTA

(Pasta Fresca)

**Makes enough long pasta for 4
(as a main, 6 as a starter)**

200 g (7 oz/1⅔ cups) '00' flour,
   plus a little extra if necessary
2 large free range eggs

---

*The standard recipe for fresh pasta
calls for 1 large egg to every 100 g
(3½ oz) of '00' flour.*

---

*For dusting use coarse semolina
as it acts like tiny ball bearings which
don't stick to the pasta.*

Fresh pasta should be made with 00 flour. This is the finest grade, according to Italian measurements, of durum wheat flour, so fine it feels and looks like talcum powder. Do buy an Italian flour, it will be superior any other kind. You can find it at Italian stores and online. The eggs should be from free-range corn-fed chickens to ensure a yellow colour and flavour. Cheap eggs and poor quality flour give anaemic and unappetising results. Eggs should be large (approx. 63–73 g/ 2–2½ oz). We keep our own chickens and sometimes their eggs can be small, so a splash of water makes up the difference in size. Some people add a little salt for flavour, some add water for elasticity or economy and some add olive oil to stop the pasta drying quickly. However, we use only eggs and flour.

Using a food processor
Put the flour and eggs into a food processor and whizz to combine just until it starts to come into a ball of dough. Tip onto the table and knead until smooth. Rest as before.

Pour the flour into a mixing bowl and make a well in the middle. Crack the eggs into the well. Using a table knife, gradually combine the flour into the eggs starting with the flour around the eggs and working your way out. Keep mixing the egg and flour until they form clumps of dough.

Use the fingertips of one hand to incorporate any remaining flour bringing everything together until you have a ball of dough. Try to squash all the crumbs of dough into the ball, but discard any that don't make it. Remove the dough from the bowl and place on a floured work surface. Knead the dough by flattening and folding it for around 5–7 minutes. Add a little more flour if it is sticky but only enough to stop it sticking to the palm of your hand. The dough should form a soft but firm ball that bounces back to the touch when prodded. If the dough becomes really dry and has many cracks in the surface wrap it in clingfilm (plastic wrap) and leave it for around 30 minutes. It will become soft and the lumps of flour will be absorbed into the egg. Failing that blitz in in a food processor with a drop of water to rescue it.

Leave the pasta to rest covered in cling film for 20 minutes at room temperature or for up to a day in the fridge. This allows the dough to relax and makes it easier to roll out through a pasta machine or by hand.

Pasta with *semola* flour

In the south of Italy pasta is often made wholly or partly with *semola di grana duro macinato*, fine semolina flour. It still comes from durum wheat but contains a little of the bran from around the outside of the wheat kernel which gives a different texture, a little more bite and creamy colour. *Semola* flour is not the same as English semolina, which is more coarsely ground and suitable only for dusting the pasta. You will find *semola* at Italian shops and on line as *semola rimacinata di grano duro*. For best results replace half of the '00' flour in the recipe above with *semola* flour.

Pasta with olive oil

Some people add oil to the dough to help its elasticity. It also makes it less likely to dry out. Add two teaspoons of extra-virgin olive oil to the dough recipe above if you would like to give it a try.

Rich egg pasta

To make rich egg pasta use, 320 g (11 oz/1⅓ cups) '00' flour, 2 whole eggs, 4 egg yolks. In the north of Italy pasta is often made with more egg yolks than whole eggs. It gives the pasta a wonderful colour and an enhanced flavour. It is the perfect match to a truffle and butter sauce. Always use corn-fed chicken's eggs to obtain the bright yellow colour. It is also a good way to use up egg yolks. Follow the method for making fresh pasta opposite.

COLOURED PASTA

Although almost undetectable in flavour, brightly coloured vegetables or natural dyes are added to pasta for dramatic results on the plate. Black pasta is made by adding ink from the cuttlefish. Spinach is used for green pasta and tomato paste for orange such as Mimmo's sunset pasta on page 154.

Beetroot pasta

Depending on the dryness of the beetroot you may need a little more flour. 300–320 g (10½–11 oz/1¼–1⅓ cups) '00' flour, 2 whole eggs and 1 egg yolk, 80 g cooked beetroot. Blend the egg with the beetroot in a food processor so that the beetroot becomes a purée. Add this mixture to the flour and follow as before.

Black pasta

Black pasta is made by adding the black ink from cuttlefish (sometimes also called squid ink) to eggs and flour when making the pasta dough. It does have a slight fishy flavour so is only used for seafood pasta recipes. The ink can vary in strength, cheaper versions being weaker so you will need to use more. As a rough guide, 2 tablespoons of ink (bought online or at good delis) is enough to colour 200 g (7 oz/1⅔ cups) '00' flour if mixed with 1 whole egg and 1 egg yolk. Whisk the ink and eggs together first before adding to the flour, following the instructions on how to make fresh pasta, left. If it looks a little grey simply add more ink and if it becomes too soft add more flour to compensate.

Spinach pasta

For the pasta: 100 g (3½ oz/½ cup) spinach, cooked from fresh or frozen and thoroughly squeezed dry, 2 egg yolks, 200 g (7 oz/ 1⅔ cups) '00' or pasta flour. To make the pasta a smooth green colour, purée the spinach in a food processor after squeezing it completely dry. If you prefer little flecks of green in the pasta, chop it by hand rather than purée it. Mix the spinach with the eggs and then add the mixture to the flour. Follow as before.

LONG PASTA

(Pasta Lunga)

To cut fresh pasta by hand

Follow the recipe for Fresh Pasta on page 26. After the resting time roll out the pasta with a rolling pin or a pasta machine to a rectangle around 14 x 30 cm (5½ x 12 in). Lightly dust the surface of the table, the pasta and the rolling pin with flour to prevent it sticking.

When it is very thin (about 1 mm thick) and you can see your fingers through it, it is ready. Dust the work surface and the pasta with plenty of flour again to prevent it sticking to itself. Gently fold over one short edge, making a flap of about 3 cm (1¼ in). Now do the same with the other short edge. Fold the edges over again and again, sprinkling flour over the surface to stop the dough sticking to itself. Stop when the folded edges meet in the middle. Cut across the folds into the desired thicknesses to make the *pasta lunga*, the thinnest being tagliolini and the fattest pappardelle. Slide a long knife underneath the centre, matching the blunt edge of the knife to where the two folded edges come together. Hold and twist the knife in the air and the pasta ribbons will fall down in cut lengths either side.

When cut, pull out into individual strands and toss with coarse semolina or a little more flour. Don't pile the pasta high but leave it in a single layer or the weight will cause it to stick together. Cook within the hour. The cooking time should be 2–3 minutes, or until al dente, in a pan of boiling salted water.

To cut fresh pasta by machine

Roll out the rested dough dusting it with semolina or '00' flour using a rolling pin or simply flatten it with your hands into a rough rectangle just wide enough to fit through the rollers of the pasta machine. Set the machine to its widest setting and roll the pasta through. Dust the pasta again and roll it through again on a notch down on the machine to reduce the gap between the rollers. Cut the length of pasta in half or quarters depending on the amount you are rolling. Repeat the dusting and rolling process again this time two notches down. Finally repeat the process on the last or the penultimate notch to obtain the required thickness of the pasta.

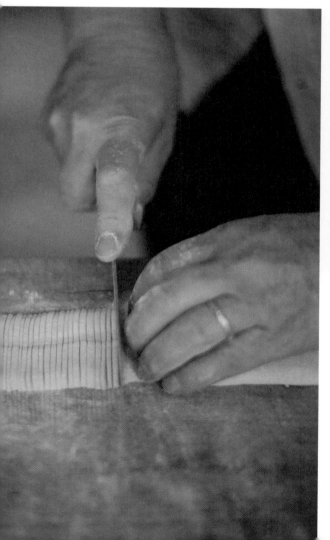

Giancarlo prefers this method of making pasta by machine; he strongly believes the pasta is better if it goes through the machine no more than 6 times as the steel rollers compress it each time and if you overdo it the texture becomes leathery. If you put the pasta through the machine as few times as possible it more like hand rolled pasta using a rolling pin.

STUFFED PASTA

There are hundreds of shapes of stuffed pasta throughout the regions of Italy, each area preferring their own traditions. By far the easiest to make is the simple square or round pillow known as ravioli or tortelli so we have given the instructions for making these. Other easy shapes are the mezzaluna on page 154 in Mimmo's sunset pasta or the cannelloni on page 120. Other folded shapes such as little hats known as cappelletti or tortelloni are harder to make and best learnt from watching an experienced hand. Don't leave fresh stuffed pasta hanging around, the filling will start to moisten the pasta and it will stick to whatever it is sitting on. Cook and serve straight away or pre-cook as per below.

We watched Vincenzo Longhitano make tortelli (pasta parcels) in the Tuscan way as he has done for 40 years. He runs the tiny trattoria in Roccatederighi in the Grosseto area. He makes his pasta fresh every day for his customers as otherwise he feels it loses its flavour and texture. He seals the tortelli with a fork so that the grooves catch the sugo (sauce). Then he cuts tagliatelle (ribbons) with a knife to show it is made by hand and not by a machine. Finally, any off-cuts are made into maltagliati (misshapen pieces). Nothing is wasted.

Pasta and gnocchi are economical to make and actually not that difficult. Over the years, Giancarlo and I have taught hundreds of people to make them in our cookery school. If you have a small pasta machine you can make and cook pasta from start to finish in 30 minutes. Stuffed pasta takes a little longer, but in this chapter we show you how to make it. As for the sauces, always have them hot and ready in a frying pan waiting for the pasta and not the other way around. If they are too dense, let them down with a little hot pasta water, or stock if you have it. Drain the pasta when it is just al dente (firm to the bite) and let it finish cooking in the sauce.

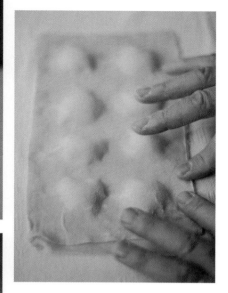

Many Italians use a ravioli mould to make stuffed pasta. If you have one follow the instructions in Rita's Ravioli (see page 122) or make by hand following these instructions.

After resting, roll out the pasta through a pasta maker using the thinnest setting so the pasta is thin but not too breakable. You should be able to see your hand or the pattern of a tablecloth through it. Lay a sheet of pasta around 40 cm (16 in) in length on to a floured worktop, keeping the top surface of the pasta flour-free. Dot heaped teaspoons, around 6–10 g (¼–½ oz) of your filling on to the sheet, 3–4 cm (1¼–1¾ in) apart to leave sufficient space to cut and seal the pasta. Now, either fold the pasta over or lay another longer sheet of pasta over the top and press around each pile of filling to squeeze the air out and seal the pasta together. Use a round cutter, the rim of a glass or a pasta wheel to cut around each piece. Lay the ravioli on to a semolina- or flour-covered tray and continue making them until you run out of stuffing.

To cut out mezzaluna – semicircles – dot the filling along the centre of a single sheet of pasta and fold it over. Press down as before to expel the air and use a wine glass or round cutter to cut out semicircles of filled pasta (see page 154).

HOW TO STORE FRESH PASTA

If you live in a warm breezy climate pasta can be dried for storage. To dry it spread out the shapes onto a tablecloth or hang ribbons over a broom handle suspended horizontally over two chairs, making sure the air can circulate around it. Once dry it can be gathered together and left in a basket until needed but take care as it will be brittle. It will keep a few days. Alternatively, you can pre-cook or freeze your pasta.

Pre-cooking pasta is a good idea if you are not going to eat it straight away. Blanch ravioli in boiling salted water for 3–4 minutes or tagliolini for 1 minute then drain and put onto a tray generously coated in sunflower oil, mixing the pasta with the oil so that it doesn't stick to itself or the tray. Allow to cool to room temperature and store in the fridge until needed. To reheat drop the pasta into salted boiling water and cook for 2 minutes for ravioli and just 30 seconds for tagliolini, or until cooked through.

To freeze pasta after part-cooking toss the shapes with a little sunflower oil and lay single layers between sheets of cling film (plastic wrap) in a container with a lid. Store for up to 3 months and cook as above.

To freeze pasta before cooking spread it out in a single layer on a tray and open freeze. As soon as it is frozen pile into bags and store for up to 3 months in the freezer. It will be fragile even when frozen so make sure it sits on top of other goods.

FABRIZIO'S HAND-ROLLED PASTA STRANDS

(Pici Alla Fabrizio)

SERVES 8

1 kg (2 lb 3 oz/8 cups)
 '00' flour
3 g (⅛ oz) salt
1 tablespoon oil
500 ml (17 fl oz/2 cups)
 cold water

Just over the border into Lazio is the small town of Cerveteri where there are a collection of Etruscan tombs. The Italians have turned these tombs into a piece of theatre as they immerse you in a recreation of Etruscan life. It is brilliant and well worth a visit. It is here that you can see a relief sculpture of what seems to be early pasta making. The Etruscans created pici, a hand-rolled pasta still massively popular today.

Fabrizio and his wife Antonella and daughter Ilaria invited us to their house to help them make ragù (see page 104) and pici. The family squabbled happily about who rolled the best pici, and after a hectic few days I felt myself finally slow down to the Tuscan pace of life. We had spent almost the whole day on one dish but what a joy it was. Not just lunch, but an invitation to partake in the skills of the Tuscan kitchen.

Put the flour in a large bowl and add the salt and oil. Add a little cold water, a splash at a time (you may not need all of it), and mix it into the flour with a wooden spoon. When the dough starts to come together and the spoon is rendered useless, put the dough onto a large wooden board and knead it with your hands. Put the crumbs into a bowl and add a splash more water. Bring that amount into a dough with your hands and then mix the two together. Add a little more flour as necessary and knead for a good 10 minutes until the ball is smooth. Wrap in cling film (plastic wrap) and leave to rest for 30 minutes. (In summer I put it in the fridge but you can leave it out in winter.)

Keep the bulk of the dough wrapped in cling film so that it doesn't dry out. Cut a palm-sized piece off and put it onto the table, then roll it out with a rolling pin to a thickness of 3 mm (⅛ in). They should be like thick spaghetti. Use a pizza cutter to cut the piece into 5 mm (¼ in) wide strips. Use your hands to roll the strips into long strands, stretching them as you roll by spreading your fingers out. Leave them separated from one another on a floured board. They can rest here for a few hours or overnight before cooking. To cook, bring a pan of salted water to the boil and cook for 8–10 minutes.

**VARIATION:
PICI WITH ANCHOVY
BREADCRUMBS**

Fry 200 g (7 oz/generous 2 cups) coarse breadcrumbs from a stale loaf with 10 salted anchovy fillets, 4 finely chopped cloves of garlic and 1 teaspoon chilli flakes in 8 tablespoons of olive oil for around 5 minutes, or until crunchy. Toss with the pici and add grated Parmesan to taste.

FRESH PASTA RIBBONS WITH HERBS & PARMESAN

(Scialatielli)

Scialatielli are a speciality of the Amalfi Coast and are made from dough mixed with either basil for a fish sauce or parsley for a meat-based sauce. They are easy and fun to make and completely satisfying to eat. Try them with with parsley for the clam sauce in the 'Ndunderi' recipe on page 147 or the sauce on page 118.

SERVES 4
(as a main, 6 as a starter)

500 g (1lb 2 oz/4 cups) '00' flour
35 g (1¼ oz) Parmesan, finely grated
225 ml (8 fl oz/1 cup) whole or
    semi-skimmed milk
1 egg
50 g (2 oz) basil or parsley,
    finely chopped

Mix the flour and cheese together in a large bowl and make a well in the centre. In a separate bowl, mix the milk and egg together and then add to the flour with the herbs. Use one hand or a dough scraper to blend the ingredients into a rough ball of dough. Turn out and knead on a floured work surface for about 5 minutes until it is smooth and well blended. Discard any dry crumbs that have not blended in. At this point the pasta can be wrapped in cling film (plastic wrap) and kept in the fridge for up to 24 hours.

Roll half the pasta out into an oval shape and push through the thickest setting of a pasta machine. Fold the ends of each strip in and push it through again. Repeat until smooth and about 3 mm (⅛ inch) thick. It should go through the rollers about 7 times. Repeat with the other half.

Cut the pasta sheets into 12 x 9 cm (5 x 3½ inch) rectangles. Flour the pieces well and put these through the tagliatelle cutter on the machine to cut into ribbons. (To do these by hand, use a rolling pin to roll out a length of pasta to the above measurements.) Dust the rectangles with flour and loosely roll up. Cut the roll into 1 cm (½ inch) wide lengths with a cook's knife then separate the strips.

The pasta should be well floured and either frozen in freezer bags or cooked within 10–15 minutes or it will become sticky. Cook in salted boiling water for 3–4 minutes and toss into the sauce to finish cooking for a couple more minutes. If cooking from frozen, allow another minute to cook.

GLUTEN-FREE FRESH PASTA

(Pasta Fresca Senza Glutine)

**Makes enough pasta for 4
(as a main, or 6 as a starter)**

50 g (2 oz/generous ¼ cup)
    gluten-free plain (all-purpose) flour
50 g (2 oz/generous ⅓ cup)
    buckwheat flour
175 g (6 oz/scant 1½ cups) tapioca
    flour (tapioca starch)
1 heaped teaspoon xantham gum
180 g (6¼ oz) egg (approximately
    3 large eggs)
1 tablespoon extra-virgin olive oil
2–3 tablespoons cold water

This recipe was first printed in our *Sicily* book as in recent years we have discovered that Giancarlo and our son Giorgio cannot tolerate wheat in their diets. This recipe was a saving grace for us. It can be used for cut ribbons as well as stuffed and shaped pasta.

Put all the ingredients, including 2 tablespoons of the cold water, into a food processor and blend until a ball of dough forms. If it is very dry and doesn't form a ball, add another tablespoon of water. You are aiming for a firm but pliable dough. Knead the dough for a few minutes to ensure it is well blended. Wrap in cling film (plastic wrap) and rest for 30 minutes at room temperature, or if you prefer to keep it longer it can be left up to 1 day in the fridge.

If you don't have a food processor, tip the dry ingredients into a bowl and stir to combine. Make a well in the centre of the ingredients and add the eggs with the oil and 2 tablespoons of water. Use a table knife to break up the eggs and combine the dry ingredients little by little. Eventually your knife will become ineffective, so use your hands to bring the dough together into a ball. If it is very dry and hard add 1 tablespoon more water. Knead and rest the dough as above.

After the dough has rested, use as fresh pasta, rolling the dough by hand or through a machine, remembering to use gluten-free flour for dusting.

QUICK PASTA RECIPES

There are many recipes for quick sauces that cook in the time it takes to cook the pasta. In the Naples area they are described as *sciué sciué*, pronounced 'shway, shway' which although sounds Chinese is actually a Neapolitan way of saying 'quick, quick'! Most sauces are made with the abundant local produce so there are many clever inventions using anchovies and lemons. Some are so simple that they are more a combination of ingredients rather than an actual recipe. Each time we spoke to an Amalfitano they would come up with yet another delicious pasta sauce, probably devised by their mother or grandmother before them.

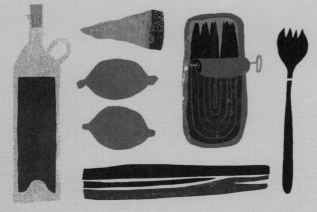

CHOVY PESTO

(ici)

Originally this pesto would have been made using a pestle and mortar but today a food processor is a quicker option. This recipe uses up the anchovies left over after making colatura di alici, a strong fish sauce made in Amalfi. We prefer salted anchovies in preference to those in oil; they should be well rinsed. If using the canned variety pour in the oil from the can too.

Put all the pesto ingredients in a food processor and blend to a runny paste. I like to leave my pesto quite rough and crunchy, but blend until smooth if you prefer. Mix in with the hot spaghetti, along with a tablespoon of cooking water to lengthen the sauce.

SERVES 8

60 g (2 oz) salted anchovies
   or anchovies in oil
50 g (2 oz) olives
50 g (2 oz) capers
30 g (1 oz) basil
1 large garlic clove
50 g (2 oz) parsley
50 g (2 oz) mixed nuts,
   such as almonds, hazelnuts,
   walnuts and pine nuts
300 ml (10 fl oz/1¼ cups)
   extra-virgin olive oil
1 small dry chilli
750 g (1lb 10 oz) spaghetti,
   to serve

Y QUICK ANCHOVY
TA SAUCES

emon, Walnut-Anchovy and Red Onion-Anchovy)

After cooking dried pasta lengths such as spaghetti or linguine, drain and toss them into a hot frying pan with extra-virgin olive oil and one of the following combinations:

Salted anchovies, freshly ground black pepper and lemon juice

Finely chopped toasted walnuts and chopped anchovies

Finely chopped fried red onion and salted anchovies

Although fish is not usually eaten with grated Parmesan

TINY FISHING BOATS GO OUT & COME IN, THE 'SPECIALS' IN THE SURROUNDING RESTAURANTS REFLECTING THE SUCCESS OF THE FISHERMEN'S CATCH

SPAGHETTI WITH GARLIC, PARSLEY & CHILLI

(Spaghetti 'Ajo e Ojo')

SERVES 4

320 g (11½ oz) spaghetti
8 tablespoons good extra-virgin olive oil
1 fat garlic clove, peeled and finely chopped
1 dried or fresh red chilli, finely chopped, to taste
salt and freshly ground black pepper
20 g (¾ oz) flat-leaf parsley, finely chopped
50 g (2 oz) pecorino or Parmesan, finely grated

This bowlful of garlicky, spicy head-tingling pasta has to be miles better than any processed food you can prepare in ten minutes. Giancarlo and his friends used to eat this after a late night working at the Rome Hilton, or even in the early hours of the morning after a night of dancing as it was quick to prepare and they always had the ingredients in the house. Its simplicity is the key to its success through generations of Italians and is summed up by the Roman proverb *'pui si mette, peggio si mangia'*: 'The more you put in, the worse you eat.'

Cook the spaghetti in a large saucepan of well-salted, boiling water according to the packet instructions until al dente. While the pasta is cooking, heat the oil in a large frying pan over a medium heat and gently fry the garlic, chilli (add more or less according to your taste), salt and pepper for 2 minutes maximum without letting it colour. Drain the spaghetti and throw it into the frying pan with the parsley and toss to combine. Serve in warm bowls sprinkled with the cheese.

SPAGHETTI WITH GARLIC, OIL, PRAWNS, LEMON & MINT

(Spaghetti 'Ajo', 'Ojo', 'Menta', Scampi e Limone)

SERVES 4
(as a main, 6 as a starter)

360 g (12½ oz) raw shell-on
   tiger prawns (shrimp)
320 g (11½ oz) spaghetti
3 tablespoons extra-virgin olive oil
1 fat garlic clove, finely chopped
4 tablespoons white wine
25 g (1 oz) salted butter
2 tablespoons finely chopped
   flat-leaf parsley, including
   thin stalks
few mint leaves, finely chopped
1 teaspoon finely grated lemon zest
fine salt

This is restaurant Pierluigi's twist on the classic *Spaghetti Ajo,*
Olio (opposite). Plump pink scampi are tossed with lemon zest
and mint leaves to create a joy to look at and a delight to eat.
If you can, try to find whole prawns with their heads still on;
the flavour with be far superior to those without. If you've made
the prawn stock on page 141, add a splash here to pep up the
flavour of the sauce.

Peel the shells off the prawns but leave the heads intact: the
flavour lies within. Use the pointed tip of a small knife to remove
the black vein from the backs of the prawns. Cook the spaghetti
in a large saucepan of well-salted boiling water according to the
packet instructions until al dente. Halfway through the cooking
time for the spaghetti, heat the oil in a large frying pan over a
medium-high heat and sauté the prawns and garlic for around
5 minutes or until the prawns turn pink and are cooked through.
Add the wine and allow to reduce for a few minutes. Add the
butter and stir through. Drain the spaghetti and toss it in the
pan with the herbs and lemon zest to combine with the sauce.

ROSCIOLI'S CARBONARA

(Carbonara di Roscioli)

SERVES 4

*250 g (9 oz) guanciale,
    or unsmoked rindless
    pancetta or streaky bacon
    plus 1 tablespoon pork fat
    or olive oil*
320 g (11½ oz) spaghetti
4 large egg yolks
1 large egg white
good pinch of salt
*1 teaspoon freshly ground
    Sarawak, Sichuan
    or black pepper*
*200 g (7 oz) Pecorino Romano
    or Parmigiano Reggiano,
    finely grated*

I have eaten a lot of carbonara in Rome in the name of perfecting this recipe, so I hope my larger dress size is worth it! Some have been too cloying, others are bland, a few tasted of cinnamon (a coating used on some cured meats) and many are served with chewy *guanciale*, the cured, fatty pork cheek that gives this dish its flavour. The best carbonara in Rome that we found was at Roscioli followed by a close second at Felice in Testaccio. Roscioli have the best *guanciale*, they use unusual crushed peppercorns and bright yellow eggs from corn-fed chickens.

Equally perfect bowls of this famous pasta can be made at home with pancetta or good-quality streaky bacon, thickly sliced from a good butcher. Make sure it is fatty and for extra flavour use a tablespoon of rendered pork fat. Alessandro Roscioli uses an iron frying pan to crisp up the cubes of *guanciale* so that they are crunchy on the outside and soft on the inside; they become like the best pork scratchings you have ever munched on, all combined with pasta in a peppery cheese coating. Incidentally, carbonara is named after the *carbonari*: the charcoal men who fed themselves on the cured meat, cheese and pasta they carried with them into the forest. Presumably black specks of charcoal are now replaced with pepper.

Cut the *guanciale* or bacon into 1 cm (½ in) cubes. Put them into a frying pan with the fat, if using (if you are using *guanciale* you won't need any extra fat), over a low heat for around 15–20 minutes or until each piece crisps up and releases its fat. Remove from the heat and set aside. Cook the spaghetti in a large pan of well-salted boiling water until al dente. While the pasta is cooking, beat the egg yolks and white together in a large bowl. Add the salt, pepper and 150 g (5 oz) of the cheese. Once the pasta is cooked, drain it into a colander and using tongs add it in 4 batches to the egg mixture, tossing it together to combine. Adding it a little at a time will prevent the eggs from scrambling. Finally, tip the bacon and fat into the bowl and toss again. Serve straight away in hot bowls scattered with the remaining cheese.

CHEESE & PEPPER PASTA

(Cacio e Pepe)

SERVES 4

3 tablespoons extra-virgin
   olive oil
1 level teaspoon freshly
   ground black pepper
320 g (11½ oz) spaghetti
1–1.2 litres (34–41 fl oz)
   boiling water
generous pinch of salt
100 g (3½ oz) Cacio de Roma
   or Pecorino Romano or
   Parmigiano Reggiano, grated

There are many ways to make this classic dish and each Roman cook will show you some slightly different way to manipulate pasta, cheese and pepper into a wonderful, warm bowl of comfort food. We saw this method, called *'risotato'* as it is like making a risotto, being used by chef Rossana Gialleonardo at Il Casaletto restaurant in the surrounding hills of Rome. After sharing her trick with us, we sat down to eat the creamiest version of *Cacio e Pepe* ever and decided from now on that is how we would do it. The pasta is cooked in a frying pan and the cooking water reduces and reduces to become the sauce. The typical Roman pasta to use for this dish is fresh *tonnarelli*, a sort of squared spaghetti, but for this method spaghetti is a must. The cheese should be the semi-soft sheep's cheese from Lazio, called *Cacio de Roma*, but if you find this hard to find use Pecorino Romano or Parmigiano Reggiano instead.

Heat the oil with the pepper in a large frying pan (around 30 cm/12 in) over a medium heat until hot and you can smell the heady spice of the pepper. Put the spaghetti into the frying pan and add 1 litre of the hot water, little by little, and the salt. Stir frequently and cook for around 10 minutes. While the pasta is cooking, warm some bowls in a low oven. If the pasta starts to look dry, add a little more water. When the water has reduced to a soupy consistency and the pasta is al dente remove the pan from the heat and add the cheese a little at a time, stirring furiously. Serve straight away in hot bowls – this is important to prevent the cheese from setting.

PASTA WITH RAW SAUCE

(Pasta Alla Checca)

SERVES 4
(as a main, 6 as a starter)

320 g (11½ oz) spaghetti
200 g (7 oz) cherry tomatoes,
* halved*
1 garlic clove, peeled and
* finely chopped*
20 g (¾ oz) capers, rinsed well
100 g (3½ oz) whole green olives,
* stones removed and quartered*
1 red chilli, finely chopped
125 g (4 oz) mozzarella, cut
* into approx. 2 cm (¾ in) cubes*
5 tablespoons extra-virgin
* olive oil*
salt and freshly ground
* black pepper*
3 tablespoons finely chopped
* flat-leaf parsley, plus extra*
* leaves, to serve*
handful of basil leaves
100 g (3½ oz) ricotta

This rainbow in a bowl is Rome's celebration of summer. Bright red cherry tomatoes are tossed with capers, olives, basil, mozzarella, chilli and garlic, and finished with ricotta. I like the raw sauce, 'checca', served with hot spaghetti but it is often served cold stirred into cooled penne for a gorgeous salad. This sauce also works well on courgetti (zucchini spaghetti).

Cook the spaghetti in a large saucepan of well-salted, boiling water according to the packet instructions until al dente. Meanwhile, gently mix the tomatoes, garlic, capers, olives, chilli, mozzarella and and oil together in a bowl. Warm a large mixing bowl ready to toss the spaghetti in. Drain the spaghetti and toss it in the warm bowl with the tomato mixture, season well and then mix in the herbs. Serve with spoonfuls of ricotta on top.

LEMON TAGLIOLINI

(Tagliolini Al Limone)

SERVES 4

1 quantity of fresh tagliolini
    made with 2 eggs and
    200 g (7 oz/1½ cups)
'00' flour (see page 26),
    or dried spaghetti or linguine
300 ml (10 fl oz/1¼ cups)
    whipping cream
juice of 1 lemon
salt and freshly ground
    black pepper
25 g (1 oz) Parmesan,
    finely grated

I would like to share with you our restaurant chef Stefano Borella's tip for making dishes with a creamy sauce: use whipping cream. Double cream such as we have in the UK or heavy cream in the US is hard to get hold of in Italy. Italians use a thinner, lighter cream called *panna da cucina*, or cooking cream. The closest we have to this is whipping cream — it has the right fat content to blend with lemon juice without splitting and yet isn't too heavy to eat in a sauce.

If using dried pasta, put this on to cook before making the sauce; if using fresh pasta make the sauce first. In a large frying pan, mix the cream, lemon juice, salt and black pepper checking for taste. Cook over a medium heat for about 5 minutes to reduce slightly and intensify the flavour. Tip the fresh pasta into the water now as it will only take a couple of minutes to cook. Drain the pasta and toss into the sauce with the Parmesan or Grana Padano. Make sure the pasta is well coated and serve immediately in warmed bowls.

FUSILLI WITH PRAWNS, WHITE BEANS & MINT

(Fusilli con Gamberetti, Cannellini e Menta)

I ate this dish on our wedding anniversary at the beautiful San Pietro hotel just outside Positano. The waiter presented me with a ring from Giancarlo, my husband, hidden under a silver salver. Continuing a perfect evening, I then ate this delicate and exciting combination of fresh green mint and sweet pink prawns against a backdrop of pale cannellini beans and homemade fusilli.

Cook the pasta in a large saucepan of well-salted, boiling water according to the packet instructions until al dente. If you are using fresh pasta, make the sauce first then cook the pasta. Drain the beans and set aside. Heat the oil in a frying pan and lightly fry the chilli and garlic with a little seasoning, being careful not to let them burn. Add the prawns and fry until pink, then stir in the beans. When the beans start sticking to the bottom of the pan, pour in the wine and alllow it to reduce for 3–4 minutes. During this time, cook the fresh pasta. Taste the sauce and season again if necessary. Scatter over the mint leaves and stir in the butter. Add the drained pasta along with a couple of tablespoons of cooking water and toss through the sauce. Serve in warmed bowls.

SERVES 4

320 g (11½ oz) dried or fresh
   fusilli (see page 52)
400 g (14 oz) cooked cannellini
   beans (either from a can
   or dried, soaked and cooked)
50 ml (2 fl oz/¼ cup) extra-virgin
   olive oil
½ red chilli, depending on strength,
   finely chopped
1 garlic clove, finely chopped
salt and freshly ground
   black pepper
16 raw tiger prawns (shrimp),
   shelled but with heads
   and tails on
100 ml (3½ fl oz/½ cup) white wine
12 mint leaves, roughly chopped
knob of butter

HOMEMADE PASTA SPIRALS

(Fusilli Fatti in Casa)

SERVES 6

300 g (10½ oz) fine
  semolina flour
3 egg yolks
50 ml (2 fl oz/¼ cup) water
1 teaspoon salt

Fusilli were supposedly created in 1550 by the chef to the Grand Duke of Tuscany. Legend says that when he was kneading the pasta he dropped a piece on the floor. To amuse himself, his son picked it up and rolled it around a knitting needle. His father was so impressed by the shape he cooked it! When times were hard the eggs were left out of this recipe but including them does improve the taste. Traditionally these shapes were made around a square length of steel called a *fuso*, but any long, thin shape will do, such as a skewer or knitting needle. This type of pasta is often made with semola *rimacinata di grano duro*, which is fine durum wheat semolina.

Pour the semolina flour into a bowl. Make a well in the centre and pour in the egg yolks and water. Use a knife to swirl the eggs and water together, incorporating the flour as you go. Gradually work this in, adding a little more water if necessary until you get a firm ball of dough. Wrap the dough in clingfilm and allow it to rest in the fridge for 30 minutes.

After this time pinch off a walnut-size piece of dough, keeping the rest covered. Over a wooden chopping board, use your palms to roll it into a length that is 5 mm (¼ inch) wide. Dust a knitting needle with flour and wind this length around it in a long spiral, then roll onto the wooden board to flatten it slightly. Gently slide it off and set aside. Repeat until you have finished the dough. The lengths can be left long, like spaghetti, or cut shorter as you wish.

Alternatively, use a pasta machine to produce 20 cm (8 inch) lengths of tagliatelle on the setting before last on the rollers. Toss them in flour. Pierce the end of a length of tagliatelle with the tip of a wooden skewer to hold it in place and gently wind it around the length of the skewer. Do not roll it flat as above, as tagliatelle are already flat, but gently ease it off the skewer and set aside on a surface dusted with flour. Cut into 3 short lengths or leave as they are.

Bring a large pan of well-salted water to the boil. Drop in the fusilli. Cook for 4–7 minutes, depending on their thickness, until they are al dente. Toss into your favourite sauce and enjoy.

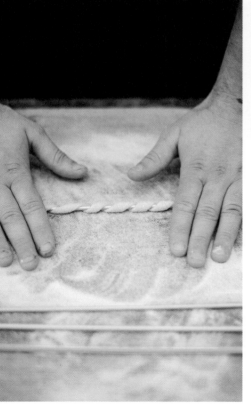

TART'S SPAGHETTI

(Puttanesca)

SERVES 4

3 tablespoons extra-virgin olive oil
1 large garlic clove, lightly crushed
½–1 fresh red chilli, finely chopped
2 heaped tablespoons black olives,
  pitted and halved
1 heaped tablespoon capers,
  drained and rinsed if salted
6 anchovy fillets
large handful of parsley,
  finely chopped
350 g (12 oz) cherry tomatoes,
  quartered
salt, if necessary
350 g (12 oz) spaghetti, to serve

It is said that the ladies of the night would make this quick sauce for extra energy using their store-cupboard ingredients. However, our friend Michelina showed us this version made with fresh cherry tomatoes rather than the canned variety. I absolutely love the punchy, spicy flavours and cook it regularly for quick lunches.

Make sure you have all the ingredients to hand and then cook the pasta in a large pan of well-salted boiling water. Heat the oil in a large frying pan and fry the garlic and chilli, followed by the olives, capers and anchovies. Stir frequently to break up the anchovies. Add the parsley and stir through. After 2 minutes, add the tomatoes. Taste the sauce and season if necessary. Cook for another couple of minutes.

When the pasta is ready, use tongs to lift it from the saucepan directly into the frying pan, along with a tablespoon of cooking water to lengthen the sauce. Serve immediately.

VARIATION

Use tinned tomatoes instead of fresh, and instead of the anchovies, gently stir through good-quality tinned tuna at the last minute.

PESTO

(Pesto)

SERVES 4–6

50 g (1¾ oz) basil, leaves
 torn from their stems
50 g (1¾ oz) pine nuts, toasted
125 ml (4⅓ fl oz/½ cup)
 extra-virgin olive oil
1 small garlic clove, peeled
25 g (scant 1 oz) Parmesan,
 finely grated

Although originally from Genoa, this sauce is now found all over Italy. Try to find Italian long pine nuts, their flavour is superior and stronger than their short counterparts from China. However pesto can also be made with different kinds of nuts, see the recipes on pages 80 and 81. For a genuine Ligurian pesto add some cooked potatoes and green beans to the pasta just before serving. Purists (and Giancarlo) will use a pestle and mortar but I prefer to use a food processor instead.

Preheat the oven to 200°C (392°F/Gas 6). Roast the pine nuts for around six minutes to bring out the flavour. Put the basil, garlic and nuts in together to blitz first. Next add the olive oil, followed by the cheese. Add salt and black pepper to taste.

Note: never heat the pesto – simply stir it into hot drained pasta instead. To keep the pesto, put it into a sterile jar and top up with a little olive oil so that the pesto is completely covered. It will last for a few days like this in a fridge.

SUMMER TOMATO SAUCE WITH PACCHERI

(Paccheri con Pomodori Freschi)

Perfectly ripe cherry, baby plum or datterini tomatoes that burst with flavour are perfect for this dish. I love to use the heirloom varieties too for a dash of colour as well as flavour. Paccheri are large open tubes of pasta commonly used on the Amalfi Coast. If you can't find them, try penne or farfalle instead. This recipe is from Michelina, the brilliant cook and owner of the beautiful Villa Maravilla in Praiano, where we shot many of the photographs for this book.

Make sure you have all the ingredients to hand and then cook the pasta in a large pan of well-salted boiling water. Heat the oil in a large frying pan and fry the garlic and chilli for 1–2 minutes, but no more as they will burn. Add the tomatoes, half the basil and some salt. Squash the tomatoes using the back of a spoon. When the pasta is just al dente, remove it with tongs and toss it into the tomato sauce, along with a tablespoon of cooking water to lengthen the sauce. Stir the pasta into the sauce and let it finish cooking – this way it will absorb more of the flavour of the sauce. Add the remaining basil and toss again. Serve in warmed bowls with a sprinkling of Parmesan or Grana Padano.

SERVES 4
(as a main, 6 as a starter)

350 g (12 oz) dried pasta, such as paccheri, penne, rigatoni or farfalle
4 tablespoons extra-virgin olive oil
1 large garlic clove, finely chopped
½–1 fresh red chilli, depending on strength, or ½ teaspoon dried chilli flakes
200 g (7 oz) fresh ripe tomatoes, roughly chopped
2 large sprigs of basil, leaves roughly torn
salt
25 g (1 oz) finely grated Parmesan or Grana Padano

*Photo shows
Pasta with
Roasted Tomatoes,
Chilli & Garlic
(recipe opposite)*

PASTA WITH ROASTED TOMATOES, CHILLI & GARLIC

(Pasta All'aglione)

SERVES 4
(as a main, 6 as a starter)

1 kg (2 lb 3 oz) cherry tomatoes,
   halved around the equator
   (not pole to pole)
7 tablespoons extra-virgin olive oil
5 garlic cloves (skin on)
a little fresh red chilli, finely sliced,
   to taste, or ¼ teaspoon dried
   chilli flakes
salt and freshly ground black pepper
1 quantity of fresh pappardelle
   (see page 26) or 320 g (11½ oz)
   dried pasta
handful of basil leaves,
   roughly torn if large
25 g (1 oz) grated Parmesan

Aglio is garlic in Italian, so aglione means 'lots of garlic', referring to the flavour of the dish. Traditionally this sauce is made from peeled plum tomatoes cooked with garlic cloves, served over thick strands of pici (see page 33). However, we like our version, which takes very little time to throw together; the tomatoes roast as you prepare the pasta and the combination is heavenly. You can serve the sauce with fresh tagliatelle or pappardelle, or dried shell-shaped pasta is good as it collects the sauce.

Don't be alarmed by the amount of olive oil. This will be the sauce when combined with the sweet juices from the tomatoes and the garlic.

Preheat the oven to 170°C (340°F/Gas 3). Put the tomatoes cut side up in a roasting tray and pour over the oil. Put the garlic cloves between the tomatoes and any tomato stems if you have them, as they will flavour the oil. Scatter with dried chilli (if using – add fresh chilli later on), season with salt and pepper, and roast for 15–20 minutes or until the tomatoes just start to collapse and brown. After 10 minutes stir the fresh chilli (if using fresh instead of dried) into the oil (fresh chilli might burn if put on top of the tomatoes at the beginning).

Meanwhile, cook the pasta to coincide with the end of the cooking time for the tomatoes (see page 19 if using dried pasta).

When the tomatoes are cooked, remove the tray from the oven and use the flat of a wooden spoon to squeeze the soft garlic out of their skins. Mix this gently with the tomatoes and discard the garlic skins as well as the tomato stems. Pour the drained pasta into the hot tray. Add the basil leaves and use a pair of tongs to combine, then serve straight away in warmed bowls, scattered with the Parmesan.

PASTA WITH CALDESI SAUCE

(Pasta al Sugo del Caldesi)

The most popular pasta at our restaurant in London, Caldesi, in Marylebone, is Giancarlo's favourite, the Linguine Caldesi. In this case, the tomato sauce on page 72 is given a touch of heat with chilli and then cooled down with double cream, before being stirred into hot linguine. Our children still love it this way, so I often make it with linguine for them and roasted vegetables for us. We often use roasted vegetables as a base for sauces in place of pasta. It makes for a lighter meal at lunchtime and is a really delicious way to eat traditional Italian sauces such tomato or ragù, if you can't eat pasta.

Heat the tomato sauce with the chilli and cream in a frying pan until bubbling and hot. Taste and season, adjusting the heat of the chilli as necessary. Meanwhile, cook the pasta according to the packet instructions (see page 19 for how to cook dried pasta) and time it so the pasta will be just cooked when the sauce is ready.

Once the sauce is ready, stir in the freshly cooked pasta and serve in warmed bowls. Dress with a swirl of good-quality olive oil, top with a basil leaf, and scatter over the grated Parmesan.

SERVES 6

1 quantity of Our Favourite
    Tomato Sauce (see page 72)
½ teaspoon dried chilli flakes
3 tablespoons double (heavy) cream
salt and freshly ground black pepper
480 g (17 oz) dried pasta, such
    as linguine
good-quality extra-virgin olive oil
a few basil leaves
25 g (1 oz) grated Parmesan

LOBSTER SPAGHETTI

(Spaghetti all'Aragosta)

SERVES 4

320 g (11½ oz) spaghetti
  or linguine
6 tablespoons extra-virgin
  olive oil
½–1 fresh red chilli, depending
  on strength, finely sliced
2 garlic cloves, lightly crushed
6 large raw prawns (shrimp),
  shelled but with heads on
1 cooked lobster, flesh removed
  and cut into bite-size pieces
salt and freshly ground black pepper
100 ml (3½ fl oz/½ cup) white wine
14 cherry tomatoes
handful of parsley, roughly
  chopped
crusty bread, to serve

As we watched the gentle waves roll into the beach at Praiano, during our research trip for the book, huge oval plates of this dish were being served at our local bar each day. The smell was fantastic. On some occasions there was no lobster because the fishermen hadn't caught any so it took us a few attempts to finally get to try this dish. Sometimes lobster can lack flavour, so we add a few prawns (shrimp).

Cook the spaghetti in a large pan of well-salted water. Meanwhile, heat half the oil in a large frying pan and briefly fry the chilli, garlic, prawns and lobster head (not the flesh), and season. Add the white wine, cherry tomatoes and half the parsley. Cover and cook for a few minutes.

　　Drain the pasta just before it is al dente and add to the frying pan to finish cooking in the sauce so that it absorbs all the flavours. Add a few spoonfuls of the cooking water if the pasta looks a little dry. Add the lobster flesh to the pan with the remaining oil and parsley. Toss together – the pasta should look 'creamy'. Serve in warmed bowls with crusty bread to mop up the juices.

CHEAT'S SPAGHETTI WITH CLAMS

(Spaghetti Alle Vongole con Pomodoro)

SERVES 4

4 tablespoons extra-virgin
   olive oil
1 x 400 g (14 oz) tin Italian
   plum tomatoes
1 x 280 g (10 oz) tin clams
   in brine, drained
320 g (11½ oz) dried spaghetti

For the Battuto
20 g (¾ oz) parsley leaves
   and fine stalks, plus a few
   more leaves, roughly
   chopped, to serve
1 small garlic clove, peeled
salt and freshly ground
   black pepper
fresh red chilli, finely chopped,
   to taste, or ¼ teaspoon
   dried chilli flakes

I was shown this cheat's version of a clam sauce by Antonella Secciani, a Tuscan chef. It uses a jar of pre-prepared clams in brine, and thought it was delicious, despite being made in just 10 minutes. This sauce works well with spaghetti or linguine. You can also reduce the sauce on the hob and serve it as a topping for polenta crostini.

Make a *battuto* with the parsley, garlic, a good pinch of salt, a generous twist of pepper and some chilli by finely chopping them together on a board with a sharp knife.

Heat the oil in a large frying pan over a gentle heat, add the battuto and fry it for about 3 minutes until the garlic is slightly golden but not burnt. Add the tomatoes and wash the tin out with approximately 100 ml (3½ fl oz/ scant ½ cup) of hot water and stir through. Break them up with a potato masher. Cook for around 20 minutes over a medium heat, adding the drained clams halfway through.

Meanwhile, cook the spaghetti according to the packet instructions (see page 19) and time it so the pasta will be just cooked when the sauce is ready. Tip the freshly cooked and drained spaghetti into the pan and toss to combine. Serve straight away with the parsley leaves.

TELL YOUR GUESTS TO EAT IT UP AS SOON AS THEY GET IT. AS GIANCARLO SAYS, 'PASTA WAITS FOR NO MAN.'

LINGUINE WITH CRAB & CREAM

(Linguine Alla Polpa di Granchio)

SERVES 4
(as a main, 6 as a starter)

3 tablespoons extra-virgin
 olive oil
15 cherry tomatoes, halved
100 g (3½ oz) brown crab meat
 and 300 g (10½ oz) white
 crab meat
100 ml (3½ fl oz/scant ½ cup)
 Prosecco or white wine
4 tablespoons double
 (heavy) cream
320 g (11½ oz) dried linguine

For the battuto
large handful of parsley,
 roughly chopped, plus
 2 tablespoons finely chopped
1 garlic clove, peeled
fresh red chilli, finely chopped,
 to taste, or ¼ teaspoon dried
 chilli flakes
salt and freshly ground
 black pepper

I always like to buy fresh crab meat when I am by the coast in the UK or Italy. The combination of a little dark meat with the white is superb and gives a richer texture and fuller flavour than the white alone. The strength of the crab can then take the kick of chilli as well as the mellowing effect of the cream. Serve this sauce with dried pasta such as linguine or with fresh tagliatelle.

Make a battuto with the 2 tablespoons of parsley, the garlic, chilli, and a pinch of salt and pepper by finely chopping them together on a board with a sharp knife.

Heat the oil in a large frying pan over a low heat and fry the battuto for 3 minutes, until the garlic just starts to soften but doesn't burn. Add the cherry tomatoes and crab meat and fry for a couple of minutes. Increase the heat and pour in the Prosecco or white wine and allow it to evaporate for a few minutes until the strong smell of alcohol has gone. Pour in the cream and shake the pan to blend it into the sauce. Taste and season with salt and pepper as necessary. Remove from the heat and set aside.

Cook the pasta until just al dente. Take 2 tablespoons of water from the pasta saucepan and add it to the sauce in the frying pan. Drain the pasta and put this in too. Add the remaining parsley and toss or stir through briefly. Serve straight away in warmed bowls.

BLACK LINGUINE WITH CRAB

(Linguine al Nero di Seppia con Granchio)

SERVES 4
(as a main, 6 as a starter)

4 tablespoons extra-virgin olive oil,
 plus more to serve
2 shallots or 1 medium white
 onion, finely chopped
1 garlic clove, finely chopped
½–1 red fresh or dried chilli,
 finely chopped, to taste
2 crabs, cooked, or 100 g (3½ oz)
 brown crabmeat and 300 g
 (10½ oz) white crabmeat
100 ml (3½ fl oz/scant ½ cup)
 Prosecco or white wine
salt and freshly-ground black
 or Szechuan pepper
1 quantity of fresh black
 or white tagliolini (see page 26-27)
 or 320 g (11¼ oz) dried black
 or white linguine

Huge spider crabs are eaten as crab salad or tossed with pasta and often served in their shells. These crabs can also be found off UK shores but we don't have a history of eating them so they are sold abroad, which is a huge shame. Their legs have an enormous amount of white, sweet meat in them. We love the crab with fresh white tagliolini served at the restaurant Antiche Carampane. Fresh pasta this thin is hard to cook perfectly so we have given the option for using dried black or white pasta. The Venetians are not big on chilli, so add or leave out as you please. Depending on whether you buy cooked crabs, their size and sex, or use pots of crabmeat you will have differing amounts of white and brown meat. Always use more white crabmeat at the end of cooking and the stronger tasting brown crabmeat in smaller amounts at the beginning. If there is red coral in the crabs, add a little of this at the end for decoration. Most Venetian kitchens have at least three types of peppercorns; my favourite with this dish is a little crushed Szechuan at the end. As chilli strength varies from chilli to chilli either add a little or a whole one. You have to be brave and taste to know!

Bring a large saucepan of well-salted water to the boil. Heat the oil in a large frying pan and fry the shallots and garlic over a low heat until softened. Add the chilli and brown crabmeat and stir through. Turn up the heat and pour in the Prosecco, allow it to evaporate until the strong smell of alcohol has gone. Taste and season the sauce. Remove from the heat and set aside. Cook the pasta until just al dente. Take a few tablespoons of water from the pasta saucepan and add it to the frying pan. Drain he pasta and put this in too. Add the white crabmeat and parsley and toss or stir through briefly. Taste once more and season further if necessary. Drizzle with your finest olive oil and serve.

SPELT SPAGHETTI WITH WILD MUSHROOMS & PARMESAN CREAM

(Spaghetti di Farro con Funghi e Crema di Parmigiano)

SERVES 4

320 g (11¼ oz) dried spelt,
  whole-wheat or white spaghetti
5 tablespoons olive oil
2 garlic cloves, peeled
  and lightly crushed
sprig of rosemary
5 sprigs of thyme
250 g (9 oz) chestnut or
  wild mushrooms such
  as chanterelles, sliced
10 g (½ oz) dried porcini soaked
  in 100 ml (3½ fl oz/scant ½ cup)
  water for 15 minutes (optional)
extra-virgin olive oil, to serve

For the Parmesan cream
 50 g (2 oz) Parmesan, finely grated
100 ml (3½ fl oz/scant ½ cup) cream

Paolo Lazzari, who runs a restaurant called Vini da Gigio, loves his food and is justly proud of his wine list. He runs the restaurant with his sister, Laura, and chef Davide. They took it on from their late parents to keep on the family tradition. Paolo is wheat intolerant so many of the dishes are low in gluten. Yet he is able to eat spelt (an ancient wheat). We tried his spelt pasta made with chanterelles and a cream of Parmesan made from the 24-month old variety, which is crumbly, dry and full of intense flavour. I really like this cheese cream and in fact it is a useful sauce for all sorts of dishes. A Venetian luxury would be to top with some shaved black truffle.

Put the spaghetti into a large pan of fiercely boiling well-salted water and stir through. Cook according to the packet instructions. Heat the oil in a frying pan over a high heat, add the garlic, rosemary and 4 sprigs of the thyme and cook for 2 minutes. If using the porcini take them out of the water when soft and slice. Add all the mushrooms to the pan and fry them for 5–7 minutes until cooked through and the water has evaporated from them. Remove the pan from the heat and discard the sprigs of rosemary and thyme. To make the cheese cream, melt the Parmesan into the cream in a small pan and keep over a very low heat.

   Drain the pasta as soon as it is ready and tip it into the mushroom mixture allowing a little of the cooking water to drip into the sauce to loosen it. Toss through and serve in warm bowls drizzled with the cheese cream, a swirl of extra-virgin olive oil and the rest of the thyme leaves pulled from the stems.

VEGETABLES/ HERBS /CHEESE

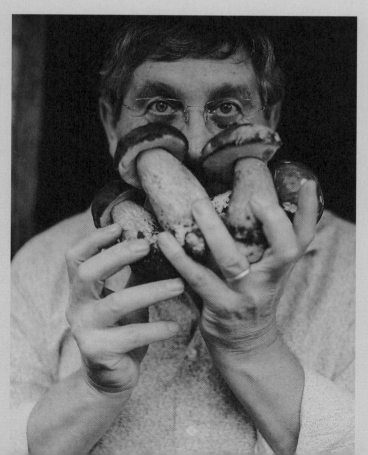

From simple chopped herbs stirred into hot spaghetti to pasta pillows stuffed with fresh ricotta, some of our favourite recipes are vegetarian. If you have leftover roast vegetables try combining them with pasta or use up seasonal gluts from the garden as a base for a sauce.

In Italy ricotta is often made from sheep's milk which gives a pleasant tang to the cheese. If you can't find this use cow's milk ricotta but always drain it before use as you don't want a watery filling.

To make a pasta salad cook dried pasta such as penne, rigatoni, orzo or shells until al dente. Drain and allow to cool in a bowl mixed with a splash of olive oil. When the pasta is at room temperature mix with a cold sauce such as Pesto on page 55, Alla Checca on page 46 or Anchovy Pesto on page 38. Serve at room temperature rather than fridge cold.

OUR FAVOURITE TOMATO SAUCE

SERVES 4–6

6 tablespoons extra-virgin olive oil
1 small red or white onion,
    finely chopped
2 garlic cloves, peeled
    and lightly crushed
1 teaspoon salt
freshly ground black pepper
2 x 400 g (14 oz) tins plum tomatoes
    (or 1 quantity Fresh Tomato
    Passata, opposite)

This is the tomato sauce that is essential to the Italian kitchen. A large jar or plastic box of it will be found in most Italian fridges. It is used on pasta, to give body to a casserole, to make eggs or to pep up a soup (I often purée it and serve it as a soup in itself). Don't skimp on the oil: if you don't use a generous amount you cannot cook the onions for long enough to get the sweetnenss out of them that balances the acidity of the tomatoes, and they would burn at the edges instead of sweating slowly and becoming translucent. Use an Italian brand of plum tomatoes – they usually taste better than from anywhere else – and always buy whole tomatoes instead of chopped, which can be watery. This sauce doesn't freeze brilliantly due to the water content but it will last up to five days in the fridge.

Heat the olive oil in a saucepan over medium heat. Add the chopped onions and garlic, then season with salt and pepper. Cook for 5–7 minutes, stirring, until the onion has softened.

Add the tomatoes and crush them in the pan with a potato masher to break them up. Rinse each tin out with a ¼ tin of cold water and add this to the saucepan. Simmer over a low heat, uncovered, for about 40 minutes. Taste the sauce and adjust the seasoning as necessary.

FRESH TOMATO PASSATA

This is Andrea Falcone's method of making a passata to use in soups. He includes the skins as this increases the flavour of the soup. You can also use it in place of tinned tomatoes when making a tomato sauce.

Preheat the oven to 200°C (400°F/Gas 6). Cut the tomatoes in half (around the equator, not pole to pole) and put them cut side up in a roasting tray. Sprinkle with salt and pepper and roast for 20 minutes or until they just start to collapse and brown. Remove from the oven and put the tomatoes in a blender or food processor. Pulse to blend, until smooth. The passata will keep for up to 4 days in the fridge.

Makes approximately 750 ml (25 fl oz/3 cups)

1 kg (2 lb 3 oz) fresh ripe,
 flavourful tomatoes
salt and freshly ground black pepper

FLAVIO'S TOMATO & PASTA SOUP

(Zuppa di Pomodoro Alla Flavio)

To make the Sugo Finto (opposite) into a soup for 4 people, add a 700 ml (24 fl oz) hot vegetable, chicken or meat stock or water to 500 ml (17 fl oz) of the sauce in a large saucepan. Bring to the boil and add 150 g (5 oz) of small pasta shapes such as *farfalline*, *stelline* or *ditalini*; stir well as they can stick to the bottom of the pan. Continue to cook over a medium heat for 5–6 minutes until the pasta is done. Check the seasoning before serving as it may need a little more salt and pepper to make up for the extra liquid. Serve in warm bowls swirled with good extra-virgin olive oil, black pepper and Parmesan. If you like it spicy, stir some crushed dried chilli into the soup as it cooks, to your taste. Flavio, who is our son, likes his special touch of a down-turned basil leaf on top. Who knows why, there's nowt as strange as kids!

ROMAN TOMATO SAUCE

(Sugo Finto)

SERVES 6

6 tablespoons extra-virgin olive oil
  or rendered pork fat
1 garlic clove, finely chopped large
sprigs basil and parsley (optional)
salt and freshly ground black pepper
3 x 400 g (14 oz) tins whole plum
  or cherry tomatoes
200 ml (7 fl oz) water or meat stock
  (optional)

For the soffritto
1 celery stick
1 medium white or red onion
1 carrot

This is so called as originally it was (and can still be) made with pork fat and meat stock, but doesn't contain any actual meat so it is a false or '*finto*' meat sauce. It is delicious in this way but if you don't have small amounts of fat and stock lying around it is just as delicious without. This make a rough-textured sauce but equally it can be put it through a *passatutto* (food mill) or blended with a stick blender to make it smooth and velvety. It turns quite bright orange in colour when blended and it's very pretty on pasta or as a soup, decorated with basil leaves and Parmesan shavings — as in the recipe opposite.

Finely chop the celery, onion and carrot by hand or in a food processor, taking care that the pieces are small — even tiny — but not puréed, to make a soffritto. Heat the oil in a medium saucepan and add the soffritto. Fry over a medium heat for about 10–15 minutes until soft. Add the garlic, herbs (if using) and salt and pepper, and fry for 1 minute to soften the garlic. Add the tomatoes and use a potato masher to mash them down. Wash each of the tins out with the water or meat stock and add this to the saucepan. Heat the tomatoes until they start to bubble then turn the heat down to a simmer and leave the sauce to cook for around 30–40 minutes, stirring frequently. Remove the herbs. Taste the sauce and add more seasoning if necessary; the sauce should be sweet from the carrots and balanced with the salt and pepper.

POOR MAN'S RAGÙ

We were shown this sauce of a reduced soffritto by Giancarlo's cousin, Tiziana Caldesi. It is known as a 'lying sauce' as it is similar to a meat ragù and was made to dress pasta when there was no meat available. It is a good vegetarian option that we sometimes serve if we are having a ragù.

Finely chop the carrot, celery, onion and parsley, by hand or in a food processor (if you use the latter, make sure you don't end up with a paste). Heat the oil in a large frying pan over a medium heat. Add the garlic, if using, and fry for 1 minute. Stir in the remaining ingredients, and season. Sweat the vegetables over a low heat, stirring and shaking the pan frequently, for 30 minutes or until the vegetables have softened. The colours will have changed from bright and sharp to soft and golden. Then add the tomato passata and cook it for a further 30 minutes. Serve the ragù with freshly cooked and drained short pasta, such as penne, and finish with a sprinkling of finely grated Parmesan.

SERVES 6–8

150 g (5 oz) carrots
  (2–3 medium carrots)
150 g (5 oz) celery (2–3 stalks),
  with a few leaves if you
  have them
150 g (5 oz) white onion
  (1 medium onion)
handful of parsley with soft
  stalks, finely chopped
150 ml (5 fl oz/⅔ cup)
  extra-virgin olive oil
fresh chilli, finely chopped,
  or dried chilli flakes, to taste
salt
400 g (14 oz) tomato passata

COURGETTE & TOMATO RAGÙ

(Ragù di Zucchine e Pomodoro)

SERVES 6

6 tablespoons extra-virgin
  olive oil
1 onion, peeled and
  roughly chopped
2 garlic cloves, peeled
  and lightly crushed
350 g (12 oz) courgettes
  (zucchini), sliced into rounds
  (a mixture of green and
  yellow, if possible)
salt and freshly ground
  black pepper
200 g (7 oz) ripe, flavourful
  tomatoes (round, cherry or
  plum), cut into 1 cm (½ in) cubes
125 g (4 oz) mozzarella,
  roughly torn
15 g (½ oz) parsley,
  roughly chopped
15 g (½ oz) basil leaves,
  roughly torn

This delicately flavoured dish is a little like a French ratatouille.
It is best made with summer produce to really appreciate the
flavours. I like to eat it in a bowl for a quick lunch or serve it as
a side dish for grilled meats. If you leave out the cheese it is
lovely with grilled fish, too. Alternatively, add a poached egg
and call it breakfast, or stir in some hot pasta shells and it will
be a perfect pasta sauce. It keeps well for a couple of days in
the fridge and is easily warmed through on the hob or in the
microwave, making it a perfect lunchtime meal.

Heat the oil in a large non-stick frying pan over a medium heat.
Add the onion and garlic and fry for about 10 minutes until the
onion is translucent. Add the diced courgettes to the pan, season
with salt and pepper, and toss through. Cook the courgettes
for a few minutes, stirring frequently, until they start to become
golden. Stir in the tomatoes and cook for a couple of minutes until
they have just begun to soften and the courgettes are al dente.
Serve straight away with freshly cooked and drained pasta shells,
while the courgettes and tomatoes are still steaming hot, topped
with the mozzarella and herbs.

PASTA WITH AUBERGINE & TOMATOES

(Pasta Alla Norma)

This glorious pasta dish was made to honour Vincenzo Bellini, the composer of the opera *Norma*, who was born in Catania in 1801. It ticks all the boxes for an outstanding dish in Sicilian cuisine; short, bouncy pasta is tossed with crispy-edged aubergine (eggplant), sweet tomato sauce, basil and salty ricotta cheese. I have used coarsely grated feta as I can't find *ricotta salata* in my local shops, but do seek it out online or in Italian delis. It has a crumbly texture and a tangy flavour. This is the way chef Roberto Toro cooked his *Pasta alla Norma* at the stunning Belmond Grand Hotel Timeo in Taormina.

Put the shallot, garlic cloves, basil sprig and olive oil together in a pan and heat gently for a couple of minutes until you can smell the flavourings. Add the tomatoes to the pan and continue to cook gently for around 20 minutes. Season to taste with salt and pepper and a little sugar if the tomatoes are too acidic. Meanwhile, heat the seed oil to around 175° C (350° F) and fry the aubergine cubes until golden. This will only take a few minutes. Scoop out the aubergines with a slotted spoon and drain on kitchen paper. Put the pasta on to cook in a large pan of boiling well-salted water. Cook until tender according to the manufacturer's suggestions. Remove the onion and garlic from the oil and discard. Add the aubergines to the sauce and stir through gently. Add the cooked, drained pasta and stir or toss again to combine. Serve in warm bowls with the feta, a few extra basil leaves, a swirl of olive oil and a twist of black pepper.

Roasted aubergines:

If you prefer not to deep-fry the aubergines, preheat the oven to 200° C (400° F/Gas 6). Toss the aubergines in a large bowl with 3 tablespoons of the olive oil and seasoning. Pour onto a tray lined with baking parchment and spread out well so they aren't piled up or they will steam. Put into the oven to roast for around 30 minutes or until they appear lightly crisp and golden brown. Add to the tomato sauce as before.

SERVES 4
(as a main, 6 as a starter)

1 small shallot, peeled but left whole

2 fat garlic cloves, peeled and crushed

1 sprig of basil, plus a small handful of basil leaves to garnish

3 tablespoons extra-virgin olive oil

1 x 400 g (14 oz) tin cherry tomatoes or 400 g (14 oz) fresh, blanched and peeled tomatoes

salt and freshly ground black pepper

1 teaspoon caster (superfine) sugar, optional

seed oil for deep-frying

1 large aubergine (eggplant), topped and tailed and cut into 2 cm (¾ in) cubes

320 g (11 oz/3 cups) pasta such as penne or spaghetti

To serve

100g (3½ oz/⅔ cup) feta cheese, coarsely grated

few extra basil leaves

extra-virgin olive oil

freshly ground black pepper

PESTO FROM TRAPANI

(Pesto Alla Trapanese)

This makes a light, delicate sauce normally used for pasta but which is also good on fried fish or spread onto hot sourdough toast. This is the way our friend Marco Piraino prepares this traditional sauce. It is usually made without the aubergines (eggplants) but we loved the extra flavour and texture they offer. Use this sauce with fresh or dried pasta. In Sicily it is often served with the curly busiate pasta.

Make a cross in the top of each tomato and then plunge them into a bowl of just-boiled water for a minute or two until the skins split. Remove from the hot water with a slotted spoon and plunge into a bowl of ice-cold water to cool for a few minutes. Meanwhile, blitz the almonds in a food processor to a gritty texture and heat enough seed oil to deep-fry the aubergine in a small saucepan.

Fry the aubergine cubes until lightly browned and then remove from the oil with a slotted spoon. Set aside to drain on kitchen paper for a few minutes to cool. Peel the skins from the tomatoes and discard the skins. Chop the flesh into small dice. Put the garlic, salt and pepper to taste, Parmesan, basil and olive oil together in a pestle and mortar. Grind until you have a rough paste, then add the almonds and tomatoes; give them a bash with the pestle then stir through. Add the aubergine last and stir to combine. Stir into hot cooked dried pasta, such as busiate (photographed opposite, bottom right).

SERVES 6
(as a main or 8 as a starter)

850 g (1 lb 13 oz) fresh
   round tomatoes
100 g (3½ oz/⅔ cup)
   blanched almonds
seed oil for frying
1 aubergine (eggplant),
   cut into 1 cm (½ in) cubes
1 garlic clove, peeled
salt and freshly ground
   black pepper
10 g (½ oz) Parmesan,
   finely grated
70 g (2¼ oz/scant 3 cups)
   basil leaves
150 ml (5 fl oz/⅔ cup)
   extra-virgin olive oil

PISTACHIO PESTO

(Pesto di Pistacchio)

SERVES 4
(makes approximately 225 g/8 oz)

100 g (3½ oz/¾ cup) shelled
  unsalted pistachios
25 g (1 oz) parsley leaves
  and stalks
1 small garlic clove, peeled
salt and freshly ground
  black pepper
100 ml (3½ fl oz/scant ½ cup)
  extra-virgin olive oil
3 tablespoons lemon juice
25 g (1 oz) finely grated Parmesan

We met a couple of passionate Sicilians selling jars of this in Ragusa Ibla. They told us you could fry some onion and bacon together and add the pistachio paste. You could also add it to a pan with sautéed prawns (shrimp), before adding pasta and little grated lemon zest. Or stir in a little cream to enrich it as a pasta sauce. I was sold and bought a jar. However, it is actually easy to make your own and you can alter the flavourings to suit. The best pistachios in Sicily come from the area of Bronte in the hills. I have found that the best flavour comes from the kind you shell at home, but I don't suggest you sit for hours slavishly picking them apart. However, a few of these, roughly chopped, on top of the pasta will enhance the taste and texture of the dish.

Put the pistachios into a food processor and grind to the texture of fine gravel. Add the remaining ingredients and whizz briefly again. Taste and adjust the seasoning. Use straight away, or store in the fridge covered with a thin layer of oil for up to a week. To use, stir into hot, just-cooked pasta.

COCOA RAVIOLI STUFFED WITH GORGONZOLA & WALNUTS

(Ravioli al Cacao Ripieni di Gorgonzola e Noci)

SERVES 6
(as a starter – makes 30 ravioli)

For the pasta
200 g (7 oz/1⅔ cups) '00' flour
2 whole eggs, plus 1 egg yolk
15 g (½ oz/2 tablespoons)
  cocoa powder
1 tablespoon water, if necessary

For the filling
50 g (2 oz/½ cup) walnuts,
  finely chopped
200 g (7 oz) gorgonzola dolce
100 g (3½ oz/⅓ cup) ricotta
30 g (1 oz) Parmesan,
  finely grated
salt and freshly ground
  black pepper

For the sauce
75 g (2½ oz/generous ½ cup)
  salted butter
1 sprig of rosemary
squeeze of lemon juice
30 g (1 oz) pecorino or Parmesan,
  finely grated, to serve

This recipe is from Ivan, the owner of Pastificio Serenissima in Castello. The cocoa gives the pasta a gorgeous nuttiness in flavour and a rich chocolate colour that contrasts brilliantly with the melting gorgonzola and crunchy walnuts inside. Try to find creamy gorgonzola dolce, which has a sweet, mellow flavor instead of the harsher crumbly gorgonzola piccante. Any leftover cocoa pasta can be rolled out again and cut into tagliatelle, which is lovely with the Parmesan Cream on page 68.

Make the pasta by following the basic fresh pasta recipe on page 84, but mix the cocoa powder into the flour first and add in the extra egg yolk. You may need to add the water if the pasta is very dry as the cocoa powder is very absorbent. Combine all the ingredients for the filling in a bowl and season to taste.

Make the ravioli by hand following the instructions for making stuffed pasta on page 30. Bring to the boil a large saucepan of well-salted water and cook the ravioli for around 5 minutes or until al dente.

To make the sauce, heat the butter in a large frying pan with the rosemary for a couple of minutes. Add a squeeze of lemon juice and shake the pan to blend it together. Discard the sprig of rosemary. Drain the pasta and add it to the pan. Shake the pan to coat the ravioli in sauce. Serve on warm plates or shallow bowls with Parmesan.

LEMON RAVIOLI IN BUTTER & MINT SAUCE

(Ravioli al Limone con Burro e Menta)

SERVES 4
(as a main, 6 as a starter –
makes 25 – 30 ravioli)

1 quantity of Fresh Pasta
   (see page 26)
coarse semolina or '00' flour,
   for dusting
a little of your best extra-virgin
   olive oil, to serve

For the filling
250 g (9 oz/1 cup) ricotta
finely grated zest of ½–1 lemon,
   plus extra to serve
salt and freshly ground
   black pepper
½ teaspoon freshly grated
   nutmeg

For the sauce
125 g (4 oz/1 stick) butter
1 tablespoon roughly chopped
   mint leaves

We watched the experienced hands of Valentina – the pasta maker at Taverna Nicastro in Modica – work her magic on a huge sheet of bright yellow pasta. Between the rhythmic movements of flouring, rolling, filling, folding and cutting, she produced puffy parcels of lemon-scented ricotta. In Sicily restaurants serve this lemony pasta with a pork ragù, which is actually just the sauce from the traditional slow-cooked ragù on page 100. It is also good with any tomato sauce. In Amalfi, these ravoili are eaten with butter and mint sauce.

Start by making the filling. Drain the ricotta then combine all the ingredients together in a bowl. Go easy on the lemon zest as it can be quite overpowering, but season generously. This is very important as you want the flavour to shine through the pasta and sauce.

Now dot a heaped teaspoon of the filling at even intervals (two fingers-width apart is ideal) on to a sheet of pasta and place another sheet of the same length over the top. Press down around the filling to expel the air and seal the pasta sheets together. Using a pasta wheel or a sharp knife, cut the ravioli into even 5 cm (2 in) squares. Set the shapes aside on a surface dusted with flour or semolina (semolina is good as it doesn't stick to the pasta).

Cook the ravioli in the boiling water for 4–6 minutes, until al dente – test by trying the edge of one. Meanwhile, make the sauce by melting the butter in a large frying pan. When the ravioli are done, drain and add to the butter in the pan with a little of the cooking water. Shake the pan to amalgamate the water and butter and add the chopped mint. Serve immediately in warmed bowls or plates.

RAVIOLI FILLED WITH TOMATO & BREAD STUFFING IN A WARM MOZZARELLA CREAM

(Ravioli Ripieni al Pomodoro in Crema di Mozzarella di Daniela Sera)

SERVES 6
(as a starter – makes 24 ravioli measuring approximately 6 cm/2½ in wide)

This is one of Daniele Sera's signature dishes that he makes at the stunning hotel Castello di Casole in central Tuscany. He has taken a typical Tuscan recipe for a tomato, basil and bread soup called *papa al pomodoro* and made it into a filling for fresh pasta. These tangy, tomatoey parcels are served in a warm bath of melted mozzarella and cream: dairy heaven in a sauce. You can enjoy it as it is or thicken with cornflour (cornstarch).

To make the filling, soak the bread in a small bowl of cold water until soaked through. Remove the bread from the bowl and squeeze out the water. Put the tomato sauce in a saucepan over a medium heat and add the bread to it – it will melt into the pan. Add the basil and stir through. Leave to cook over a low heat for 15 minutes or until the bread has broken down and thickened the sauce. Remove from the heat, transfer to a bowl and allow to cool to room temperature.

Dot heaped teaspoons of the filling at even intervals (two fingers' width apart is ideal) onto one of the sheets and place another sheet of the same length over the top. Press down around the filling to expel the air and seal the pasta sheets together. Using a pasta wheel or a sharp knife, cut the ravioli into even 5 cm (2 in) squares. Set the shapes aside on a surface dusted with flour or semolina (semolina is good as it doesn't stick to the pasta). Repeat with the remaining pasta until the filling is used up.

For the mozzarella cream, put the mozzarella, the brine from the bag, the cream and butter into a saucepan and set over a high heat to melt. When the cheese has melted pass it through a sieve to remove any remaining small lumps of cheese. Taste and add salt as necessary.

To serve, warm the mozzarella cream sauce over a gentle heat. Drop the pasta into well-salted boiling water and cook for 2–3 minutes. Drain and put into a warm dish with the butter and toss to combine – this will stop the pasta sticking. Put a ladleful of mozzarella cream into each bowl and place the pasta on top. Drizzle olive oil on top of each dish, sprinkle over a little grated Parmesan, season with black pepper and serve straight away.

For the filling
50 g (2 oz) stale country-style bread
150 ml (5 fl oz/⅔ cup) Our Favourite Tomato Sauce (see page 72)
10 g (½ oz) basil leaves, roughly chopped

For the ravioli
1 quantity of Fresh Pasta (see page 26)
coarse semolina or '00' flour, for dusting

For the mozzarella cream
1 x 125 g (4 oz) ball of mozzarella, roughly chopped, plus the water/brine from the bag
125 ml (4 fl oz/½ cup) double (heavy) cream
125 g (4 oz) unsalted butter
salt, to taste

To serve
25 g (1 oz) salted or unsalted butter, cubed
extra-virgin olive oil, for drizzling
25 g (1 oz) grated Parmesan
freshly ground black pepper

RAVIOLI STUFFED WITH POTATO & CHEESE

(Ravioli di Mugello)

Makes 200 g (7 oz) filling for
36–40 (4 cm/1½ in square) ravioli

For the filling
200 g (7 oz) fluffy potatoes
  such as King Edward or
  Desiree, unpeeled
1 small garlic clove, peeled
5 g (¼ oz) parsley
generous pinch of finely
  grated nutmeg
½ teaspoon salt
35 g (1¼ oz) grated Parmesan
freshly ground black pepper

For the ravioli
1 quantity of Fresh Pasta
  (see page 26)
coarse semolina or '00' flour,
  for dusting

This recipe is from our friend Franca Buonamici. Mugello is a small town in the north of Tuscany and their recipe for these soft pillows of pasta filled with potato and cheese has become famous. Any leftover stuffing can be made into small patties and fried in oil. These are ideal to serve with a ragù such as the Duck Ragù on page 116.

To make the filling, bring a large pan of salted water to the boil, add the potatoes and cook them in their skins until tender. It will take up to 1 hour for large ones, but don't be tempted to cut them up or they become watery. Traditionally, they are always boiled, but they are also good pierced with a fork a few times and baked or cooked in a microwave. Meanwhile, finely cut the garlic and parsley together on a board.

When the potatoes are cooked through, drain and peel them while they are still hot by holding a potato in one hand with a cloth or a fork and peeling or scraping away its skin with a knife. Ideally, pass the potatoes through a ricer, sieve or food mill into a bowl (if you don't have any of those, use a masher). Mix in the garlic, parsley, nutmeg, Parmesan, salt and a good twist of pepper. Taste and adjust the seasoning as necessary. The filling should have a fairly strong flavour as it needs to be detectable through the pasta and sauce. To make the ravioli, follow the instructions for making stuffed pasta on page 30. Serve tossed in a pan with warm Duck Ragù (see page 116).

LARGE RAVIOLI FILLED WITH SPINACH & EGG YOLK

(Cappelli di Frate)

These large filled ravioli (*cappelli di frate*), named after the shape of a monk's hat, make a stunning dinner party dish as the egg yolk oozes out as you eat them. We use an 11 cm (4¼ in) pastry cutter but you could instead draw a knife around a small 10–12 cm (4–5 in) diameter saucer to make the circles of pasta.

To make the filling. Finely chop the cooked spinach on a chopping board or in a food processor. Mix in a bowl with the ricotta, Parmesan, nutmeg, salt and pepper. Adjust the seasoning as necessary. Cover and set aside until required.

Roll out half the pasta at a time, following the instructions on page 26 to the width of the pasta machine. Lay the first sheet onto a floured board and cut the length in half. Don't get flour onto the pasta on the top side. Use an 11 cm (4¼ in) cutter to lightly make 3 circles – these will be the size of your finished *cappelli del frate*. Use a spoon to place 3 equal heaps of half of the filling into the circles. Lightly press the filling outwards leaving a 1 cm (½ in) border around each mound with a well in each one large enough for the yolk. Put 1 egg yolk or 1 quail's egg into each well. Lay the other length of pasta on top and press down, pushing out the air and sealing the edges down. You shouldn't need water to stick the pasta together, but if it is dry, brush lightly with water to help it stick. Use your cutter to cut through the layers of pasta. Set aside on a floured plate and make up the rest. Leave on a floured plate for no longer than 2 hours in the fridge.

To cook, bring a large pan of salted water to a rolling boil. Make the sauce by melting the butter in a large frying pan. Add the sage leaves, a pinch of salt, pepper, pine nuts and fry for a couple of minutes. Add a ladleful of pasta cooking water and stir. Keep the sauce warm but not bubbling while you cook the pasta.

Gently lower the ravioli into the boiling water, and stir gently to make sure they don't stick together. Cook for 4 minutes for a soft yolk and 6 minutes for firm. When cooked, remove the ravioli gently with a slotted spoon and put them into the warm butter and sage sauce. Shake the pan to coat the pasta and serve immediately in warm bowls with the sauce and grated Parmesan.

SERVES 6

For the filling
200 g (7 oz) spinach, cooked and squeezed dry
30 g (1 oz /⅛ cup) fresh ricotta
30 g (1 oz) grated Parmesan, plus extra to serve
¼ teaspoon freshly grated nutmeg
¼ teaspoon salt
freshly ground black pepper, to taste
6 egg yolks or 6 quail's eggs
25 g (1 oz) grated Parmesan, to serve

For the ravioli
1 quantity Fresh Pasta (see page 26)
coarse semolina or '00' flour, for dusting

For the sauce
150 g (5 oz) salted butter
18–20 sage leaves
salt and freshly ground black pepper
30 g (1 oz) pine nuts, toasted

CHEESE FILLED RAVIOLI IN SAFFRON & HERB SAUCE

(Raffioli de Herbe)

SERVES 4
(as a main, 6 as a starter)

1 quantity Fresh Pasta (see page 26)

For the filling
200 ml (7 fl oz/scant 1 cup) milk
50 g (2 oz/scant ½ cup) '00' flour
100 g (3½ oz) cheese such as
   pecorino, fontina or asiago
60 g soft goats' cheese
50 g (2 oz) Parmesan or grana
   padano, finely grated
salt and freshly ground
   black pepper
2 egg yolks

For the sauce
50 g (2 oz/½ stick) salted butter
2 tablespoons extra-virgin olive oil
2 celery stalk with leaves, chopped
2 leeks, chopped
1 litre (34 fl oz) vegetable stock
   (or chicken stock)
1 heaped teaspoon grated
   fresh ginger
½ teaspoon saffron
salt and freshly ground
   black pepper

To serve
50 g (2 oz/½ stick) salted butter
large handful of aromatic leaves
   such as rosemary, thyme, sage
   or marjoram
30 g (1 oz) toasted flaked
   (slivered) almonds
30 g (1 oz) smoked cheese such
   as ricotta, scamorza or smoked
   Cheddar, coarsely grated

This is a stunning dish to serve. The plump ravioli are filled with three kinds of cheese, bathed in glorious saffron sauce and decorated with aromatic leaves. The recipe is an adaption of the original by the Anonimo Veneziano from the 1300s, created by Sergio and Mario at the restaurant Bistrot de Venice where it forms part of their historical Venetian menu.

For the filling heat the milk in a medium saucepan over a medium heat, whisk in the flour and continue whisking over the heat until thick and any lumps have disappeared. Turn the heat to low and add the cheeses, season and whisk through. Take the pan off the heat and whisk in the egg yolks. Taste and adjust the seasoning as necessary, allow to cool to room temperature.

Prepare and fill the pasta according to the instructions on page 122 using 10 g (½ oz) of filling per raviolo and using a 6 cm (2½ in) cutter or wine glass to cut the pasta. To make the sauce, in a large frying pan heat the butter and oil and fry the celery and leeks over a medium heat until softened. Add the stock, ginger, saffron and seasoning, turn up the heat and bring to the boil. Reduce the heat and simmer gently for 15 minutes. Taste and adjust the seasoning as necessary. Purée the sauce in a blender and set aside.

To assemble the dish, melt the butter in a frying pan and add the herbs. Fry them for around 2 minutes, take off the heat and set aside. Bring to the boil a large saucepan of well-salted water and cook the ravioli for around 5 minutes or until al dente. Reheat the sauce in a large saucepan and add the drained pasta to it. Arrange the ravioli on each plate with a little of the sauce poured over the top. Drizzle the herby butter around the plate. Scatter over the flaked almonds and grated cheese, then stand back and admire your work!

HALF MOONS OF PASTA FILLED WITH BEETROOT IN POPPYSEED BUTTER

SERVES 4

(Casunziei Amperzzani)

1½ quantity Fresh Pasta
  (see page 26)

For the filling
250 g (9 oz) cooked beetroot
100 g (3½ oz) cooked potato
100 g (3½ oz/1¼ cups)
  fresh breadcrumbs
2 egg yolks
¼ teaspoon ground nutmeg
½ teaspoon fine salt
freshly ground black pepper

For the sauce
100 g (3½ oz/scant ½ cup)
  salted butter
¼ teaspoon ground cinnamon

To serve
 1–2 teaspoon poppy seeds
30 g (1 oz) Parmesan
  or smoked cheese, shaved

This is a traditional dish of the skiing area of Cortina in the Dolomites. We love this pretty dish of half moon shaped pasta filled with pink beetroot stuffing and served with poppy seeds and butter. They should be served just coated in butter rather than enjoying a swim in it.

To make the filling blend the beetroot and potato in a food processor, or mash by hand, until smooth. Transfer to a mixing bowl and stir in the breadcrumbs, egg yolks, nutmeg, salt and season with pepper to taste. Prepare and stuff the pasta following the instructions for agnolotti (see page 154) using a 6 cm (2½ in) round cutter or large wine glass to cut out the half moon shapes.

Melt the butter with the cinnamon in a large saucepan then turn off the heat so you don't burn the butter. Bring a large saucepan of salted water to the boil and cook the half moons for 5–6 minutes until al dente. Drain the pasta and add to the butter in the pan. Shake the pan so that the *mezzaluna* become coated in butter. Serve in warm shallow bowls and scatter with poppy seeds and Parmesan.

MEAT/ POULTRY /GAME

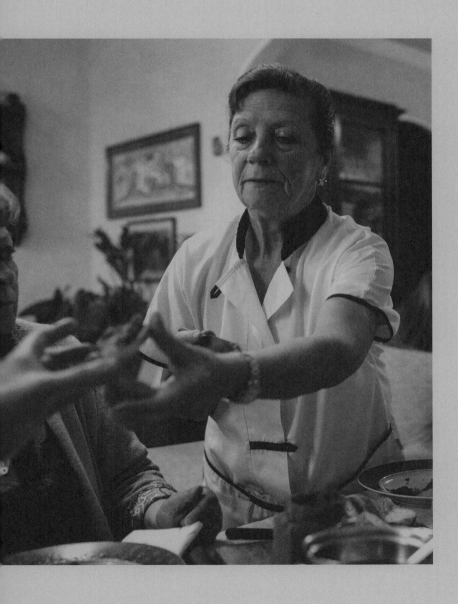

These recipes take a little longer to prepare but are well worth the effort. Many can be frozen, so it's a good idea to make an extra-large batch for another day. A slow cooker is very useful for making sauces such as ragù as you can leave them to bubble away gently while you get on with other things. When making fresh pasta it's a good idea to enlist the help of friends or family. I was once told that making pasta isn't just about lunch; it's really about making time to catch up with others and giving yourself time to chat. I like that idea.

MEMMO'S BEEF RAGÙ

(Ragù di Memmo)

SERVES 16–20

For the soffrito
200 g (7 oz) carrots
200 g (7 oz) celery stalks
200 g (7 oz) red or white
  onions, peeled
3 garlic cloves, peeled
2 sprigs of rosemary
100 ml (3½ fl oz/scant ½ cup)
  extra-virgin olive oil
salt and freshly ground
black pepper

For the ragù
2 kg (4 lb 6 oz) beef, coarsely
  minced (ground)
500 ml (17 fl oz/2¼ cups) red wine
1.2 kg (2 lb 10 oz) tinned plum
  tomatoes

Tuscan meat ragù is rich and herby in flavour compared to its neighbouring Bolognese ragù, which usually contains no herbs or garlic. We always make a lot of this when we cook it as it freezes well. Giancarlo's father, Memmo, used to make it every 14 days, and he would pour it into glass jars and store it in the fridge. Every day at 1 pm he would unscrew a jar and warm it up to have with his pasta. For two weeks he had an easy lunch before he made the next batch. We ask our local butcher to give us a fatty cut of beef, around 15 per cent fat, and coarsely grind the meat for us. Giancarlo's family ate this ragù with fresh fettucine or dried pasta such as spaghetti, but it is also lovely on soft cheesy polenta or roasted vegetables.

In a large frying pan (skillet), make a soffritto with the carrots, celery, onions, garlic, rosemary, oil and seasoning, but finely chop the garlic with the other vegetables. When the soffritto is soft, remove the rosemary sprigs.

To make the ragù, add the mince to the soffritto and stir well. Cook the for around 20 minutes, stirring frequently and allowing the water to evaporate from the pan. Add the wine and let it reduce until the smell of alcohol dissipates. Pour the tomatoes into a bowl and crush them with your hands (this is Giancarlo's way; my way is to use a potato masher when they are in the pan – the choice is yours!). Add the tomatoes to the pan, stir and bring to the boil. Turn down the heat and continue to cook for around 2 hours, uncovered, over a low heat. If the heat is low, it shouldn't catch, but do keep an eye on it and add a little hot water if it looks dry. Taste and adjust the seasoning.

Use straight away or allow to cool and store in the fridge in a covered container for 1 week, or freeze for up to 3 months.

SICILIAN RAGÙ

(Ragù alla Siciliana)

425 g (15 oz) Italian sausages
325 g (11½ oz) pork spare ribs
425 g (15 oz) pork belly, cut
   into 3 cm (1¼ in) cubes
425 g (15 oz) stewing beef,
   cut into 8 cm (3¼ in) chunks
5 tablespoons extra-virgin
   olive oil
2 white or brown onions,
   finely chopped
3 garlic cloves, peeled
   and roughly chopped
2 bay leaves
1 sprig of rosemary
salt and freshly ground
   black pepper
300 ml (10 fl oz/1¼ cups)
   white or red wine
4 tablespoons tomato purée
   (tomato paste)
1.2 kg (2 lb 10 oz) tinned whole
   tomatoes, roughly chopped
1 litre (34 fl oz/4¼ cups) chicken,
   meat or vegetable stock,
   or hot water
6 potatoes (approximately 1 kg/
   2 lb 3 oz), peeled and cut in half
200 g (7 oz/1⅓ cups) peas,
   frozen or fresh (optional)

Traditionally, ragù was made on a Sunday and normally it would be the mamma of the house who would get up early to get it started over a fire, so that it would be ready in time for a late lunch. Nowadays, with slow cookers and heavy, cast-iron casseroles like Le Creuset you can get it going, turn the oven on low and go out for the day. You will come back to a heavenly feast that is the wonderfully rich and sticky ragù ready to cling to pasta shapes or gnocchi.

We tested this recipe at our restaurant in Bray. A couple of the staff are Sicilian and they ate it for their dinner. They loved it and actually became quite emotional! I think we got pretty close to the original recipe. Don't worry if you don't have all the types of meat – it really should be made with what you have to hand, so use more beef or pork accordingly. Do try to find proper Italian sausages, though, as they are full of flavour from garlic, wine and sometimes fennel seeds and don't contain rusk. Serve this with dried or fresh long pasta.

Brown the meat in batches in the oil in a large casserole dish over a medium heat, setting it aside in a large bowl when done. Add the onions to the pan in the remaining oil with the garlic, bay leaves, rosemary and seasoning and cook over a gentle heat to soften. It should take 7–10 minutes. Add the meat back into the pan with the wine and bring to the boil. Allow to reduce for few minutes. Add the tomato purée, tomatoes and stock and stir to combine. Bring to the boil, then reduce the heat to a simmer and allow to cook slowly for 4–5 hours. The time will depend upon the cut of meat and the size. You need to cook it until the meat falls easily from the bones. Add the potatoes after around 4 hours and continue to cook until they are cooked through. Add the peas, if using, towards the end of the cooking time. Cook for 15 minutes if using frozen peas and 30 minutes if using fresh ones. Taste and adjust the seasoning as necessary. Eat the stew as it is or ladle off most of the sauce and serve it with pasta, followed by the meat and potatoes as a main course served with the purple sprouting broccoli.

NEAPOLITAN RAGÙ

(Ragù alla Napoletana)

All Neapolitan mammas have their own recipe for this intense, rich sauce. In fact it is more of a stew than a sauce as it contains roughly cut cubes or whole pieces of beef, often pork ribs and sometimes sausages. When the sauce is cooked, the tomato is spooned off from the meat and eaten with pasta for a first course, while the meat is served as a main course with vegetables. Old cookbooks dictate that ragù should be cooked for a whole day and many cooks still do this, which results in a glorious beefy tomato sauce. It is for this reason that the quantity of canned tomatoes is huge as they reduce during cooking. Many Amalfitani originate from Naples and have never had any reason to change the recipe. Ours is from our Neapolitan sous-chef Marco di Simone, who got it from his mother, who in turn got it from hers.

A *soffritto* is a lightly fried mixture of vegetables, usually carrots, celery and onions, used as a base for ragù, stews and soups, providing a little sweetness to counteract the acidity of the tomatoes. The vegetables can be chopped by hand or very briefly whizzed in a food processor.

Start by making the soffritto. Heat the oil in a large heavy-based saucepan. Fry the carrots, onion, celery, bay leaves and garlic over a medium heat for 15–20 minutes, or until soft. Add the sausages, ribs and beef with the salt and black pepper. Brown the meat on all sides then add the wine and allow it to reduce for about 5 minutes, until the sauce is really dark and the wine has almost evaporated (I am often tempted to start eating it at this point as it smells so delicious!) Add the passata and the tomato purée and bring to the boil. As soon as the sauce starts bubbling, cover the pan and lower the heat. Cook on a low heat for 5 hours, or 8 hours if you can manage it, stirring every so often. Keep an eye on the sauce and add a little hot water if starts to look dry.

SERVES 8–10

200 ml (7 fl oz/scant 1 cup)
  extra-virgin olive oil
3 large carrots, finely chopped
1 large white onion, finely chopped
3 celery stalks, finely chopped
4 bay leaves
3 large garlic cloves, lightly crushed
6 Italian sausages
350 g (12 oz) pork ribs,
  cut into individual ribs
500 g (1 lb 2 oz) top rump
  or blade steak, cut into 4 cm
  (1½ inch) chunks
2 teaspoons salt
1 teaspoon freshly ground
  black pepper
200 ml (7 fl oz/scant 1 cup) red wine
2.5 kg (5½ lb) tomato passata
  (see page 73) or broken-up
  tinned whole tomatoes
3 tablespoons tomato purée

WOOD PIGEON RAGÙ WITH PICI

(Ragù al Colombaccio con Pici)

Fabrizio Biagi was a hunter and made pici, the hand-rolled pasta, to go with ragù made from his catch. Now his time is taken up cooking and painting so he leaves the hunting to other men.

Fabrizio showed me the juniper berries that he collected in the woods nearby. Apparently they are harvested in an upturned umbrella – the locals bang the branches and the berries fall into it. Antonella took me to the window and pointed out where the pigeons came from on a nearby farm as well as the olive trees that provided the cooking oil. Between them they could point out the provenance of nearly everything we were about to eat.

The ragù, also known as *ragù dell'aia* (meaning what was roaming around the farmyard earlier!), works for other birds such as pheasant, quails or partridge, as well as other types of pasta. My favourite is fresh pappardelle or, if using dried pasta, spaghetti would work well. Fabrizio feels that the time, wine and *aroma* (flavourings) used for marinating are the most important part as the flavour is developed then. He likes to use a local Chianti wine.

Wash the pigeons in cold water to get rid of the blood, then dry them with a clean towel. Put them in a large bowl with all the marinade ingredients and leave them to marinate in the fridge for 1–2 hours.

Meanwhile, make the *battuto* by using a mezzaluna or a sharp knife to finely chop the ingredients together. After the birds have marinated, drain them, keeping the marinade and fishing out the vegetables. Put the pigeons onto paper towel to dry it out or, as Fabrizio kept saying, *scollare bene* (pat dry with the towel). Season them with the salt and pepper.

SERVES 8

For the pigeon
4 pigeons, approximately
    175 g (6 oz) each, quartered
    (with the giblets left in)
2 teaspoons salt
½ teaspoon freshly
    ground black pepper
120 ml (4 fl oz/½ cup) extra-virgin
    olive oil
3 slices of rigatino or unsmoked
    bacon, roughly chopped
500 ml (17 fl oz/2¼ cups)
    beef bone broth
Fabrizio's Hand-Rolled Pasta
    Strands (see page 33),
    to serve (optional)

For the marinade
½ red onion, peeled and
    roughly sliced into wedges
small handful of parsley
handful of sage leaves
2 bay leaves
5 sprigs of rosemary
15 juniper berries
fresh red chilli, to taste
2 celery stalks
1 carrot
750 ml (25 fl oz/3 cups)
    red wine

For the battuto
small handful of sage leaves
2 sprigs of rosemary,
    leaves picked
1 fat garlic clove

Put the oil in a large pan over a medium heat and, when hot, saute the birds with the *battuto*. Brown them all over for about 10 minutes. Wash the vegetables from the marinade briefly in cold water, cut them into small pieces, then add them to the pan with the rigatino or bacon. Fry for 10–15 minutes or until soft. Add 200 ml (7 fl oz/generous ¾ cup) of the marinade. Cook over a medium heat until the scent of wine has disappeared and the sauce has reduced. Pour in the stock to almost cover the meat. Bring to the boil and cover the pan.

Reduce the heat and simmer for 1–1½ hours or until the meat falls from the bones. Remove from the heat and leave until the pigeon is cool enough to touch. Pick the meat and skin from the bones, taking care to remove and discard any small bones. Chop the meat finely on a board with a large cook's knife or mezzaluna. Put this chopped mixture back into the pan and reheat to further reduce the sauce. If it looks dry, add a little hot water.

Meanwhile, if using, cook the pici (see page 33) in plenty of salted boiling water with a dash of oil until al dente. They will take 7–10 minutes, depending on their size. Drain and toss into the pan to combine with the sauce. Serve in warm bowls straight away.

SAUSAGE & WILD FENNEL RAGÙ

(Ragù di Salsicce e Finocchio Selvatici)

SERVES 4
(as a main, or 6 as a starter)

Wild fennel grows everywhere but most of us ignore it. It sprouts up merrily in early spring in the UK; it is bright green and feathery, then becomes darker over the months and finally blossoms into yellow flowers that yield the seeds in autumn. Do seek it out; you can usually find it in hedgerows, or use fennel seeds instead. Fresh ricotta is often stirred into hot pasta in Sicily; sometimes it can be dry, in which case stir in a little cream at the same time.

Heat the oil in a large frying pan and fry the leek for around 5 minutes. Meanwhile, squeeze the sausage meat from the skins and crumble it into the pan with the leek. Fry over a medium to low heat until the meat is browned. Add the red wine and let it evaporate for around 5 minutes, then stir in the wild fennel (keep a little for garnish) and some pepper. Let the ragù cook slowly over a low heat for around 30 minutes. Taste and add a little salt if necessary (Italian sausages tend to be quite salty so go easy). Just before serving, stir in the ricotta and cream, if using, then add just-cooked pasta to the pan. Stir through and serve garnished with the reserved fennel and, if liked, some Parmesan on top.

4 tablespoons extra-virgin olive oil
½ large leek (about 150 g/5 oz), trimmed and finely chopped
500 g (1 lb 2 oz) Italian rusk-free sausages
5 tablespoons red wine
small handful (25 g/1 oz) of wild fennel, finely chopped, or 1 teaspoon fennel seeds
salt and freshly ground black pepper
100 g (3½ oz/generous ⅓ cup) ricotta
75 ml (2½ fl oz/⅓ cup) double (heavy) cream (optional)
25 g (1 oz) finely grated Parmesan (optional)

BOLOGNESE RAGÙ

(Ragù alla Bolognese)

This recipe comes from our book *The Italian Cookery Course*; I wrote it after a trip to Bologna to find the quintessential *Ragù alla Bolognese*. Of course there is no such thing as all Bolognese cooks make it in a slightly different way. However many used chicken livers and most finished the sauce with milk. It is good to note that it is definitely a meat sauce with a little tomato rather than the other way around.

Outside Italy a *'Bolognese'* has become shorthand for saying 'meat sauce' but in Italy a meat sauce is a 'ragù' and it is usually followed by the area the sauce comes from hence *'Ragù alla Bolognese'* or *'Ragù alla Siciliana'* for example.

Make the soffrito by gently frying the vegetables in hot oil for 15–20 minutes or until softened. Add the mince, pancetta and chicken livers and fry for 10–15 minutes over a medium heat, stirring frequently until the meat is browned and the water has been released and evaporated. The mixture should be sizzling as it is stirred. Add the wine and cook over a high heat for 5 minutes until the wine has separated from the oil. At this point add the tomatoes, rinsing out the cans with the stock, and add this too. Turn down to a simmer and leave to cook for 1 hour. Add the milk and stir through, leave to cook for a further 30 minutes. Adjust the seasoning to taste.

SERVES 8
(as a main, 10 as a starter)

1 quantity of soffrito
(see the Sugo Finto recipe
on page 75, omitting the
garlic and rosemary
600 g (21 oz) beef mince
200 g (7 oz) pancetta or unsmoked
streaky bacon, minced in a food
processor or cut finely by hand
200 g (7 oz) chicken livers,
chopped finely
400 ml (13½ fl oz/1½ cups) red wine
2 x 400 g (14 oz) tins of tomatoes
200 ml (6¾ fl oz/¾ cup) meat stock
used to rinse out the tins
150 ml (5 fl oz/½ cup) milk
1 teaspoon salt

LASAGNE

SERVES 10–12

*1 quantity of pasta made with
   2 eggs and 200g '00' flour,
   see page 26.*
*1 quantity of béchamel sauce,
   see below*
*1 quantity of Ragù alla Bolognese
   on page 108 or half the quantity
   of Memmo's ragù on page 99*
100g (3½ oz) Parmesan, finely grated

For the béchamel
(Makes 1.5 litres (51 fl oz/6 cups))
1.5 litres (51 fl oz/6 cups) milk
*1 small onion, peeled
   and cut in half*
2 bay leaves
¼ nutmeg, finely grated
100 g (3½ oz) butter
100 g '00' (3½ oz) flour
Salt and black pepper to taste

VARIATIONS:

To further enrich the lasagne
add soaked Porcini mushrooms
(25g (1 oz) dry weight) to the ragù.

Tear 250g (9 oz) of mozzarella into
bitesize pieces and add between
the layers.

For a vegetarian version use
roasted vegetables and tomato
sauce instead of the ragù.

**From an endless list of possible ways to make lasagne this is our
favourite. It is the way Giancarlo's mother used to make it and
the way we have taught our children to make it and who in turn
I hope will one day keep the tradition going. The importance,
as Giancarlo will stress, is that the ends of the pasta are exposed
in places to the heat of the oven rendering them crispy. There
are not many layers, ensuring the dish is light. The sauces are
'dolloped' between the layers and not mixed uniformly together
first so that each mouthful is slightly different.**

Make and cook the pasta sheets according to the recipe for
Cannelloni on page 120. If using dried pasta, precook as required,
following the manufacturer's instructions.

    Preheat the oven to 180°C (350°F/gas mark 4). Drop spoonfuls
of béchamel and ragù into a lasagne dish measuring 25 x 32 cm
(10 x 12½ in). Scatter with a little Parmesan. Next make a layer of
cooked lasagne sheets, avoiding them overlapping. Repeat the
spoonfuls of béchamel and ragù, Parmesan and pasta sheets
and continue to build up about three layers in this way, finishing
with the sauces. Scatter with the remaining Parmesan and
transfer to the oven for around 30–40 minutes or until golden
brown on top and bubbling at the edges.

Béchamel Sauce
Bechamel should always be a delicious, tasty sauce. So do use
the flavourings above, it will all add to the richness of the dish.
The Italian way is to put the roux (butter and flour) into the milk
all in one go. It's easy and never goes lumpy.

    Put the milk, flavourings and seasoning into a medium
saucepan over the heat and bring to a gentle boil. Meanwhile
make a roux: melt the butter in a small saucepan and stir in the
flour. Cook for a few minutes, stirring constantly. Remove the bay
leaves and onion from the milk and add the roux while whisking
furiously. Cook until it thickens, adjust the seasoning and remove
from the heat. Cover the surface with cling film (plastic wrap)
or a circle of damp baking parchment to prevent a skin.

LAMB RAGÙ WITH SPICES

(Ragù di Agnello Speziato)

SERVES 6–8

1¼ kg (2 lb 12 oz) lamb shoulder,
  diced into 2 cm (¾ in) cubes
4 tablespoons extra-virgin olive oil
200 g (7 oz) leeks, finely chopped
1 garlic clove, lightly crushed
7 cloves, ground
salt and freshly ground
  black pepper
3 cm (1¼ in) cinnamon stick
200 ml (7 fl oz/scant 1 cup)
  white wine
750 ml (25 fl oz) beef stock
  (bouillon) (chicken or vegetable
  would also work)
Parmesan, finely grated to serve

For the bouquet garni
4 large sage leaves
5 short sprigs of thyme
1 long sprig of rosemary,
  cut into pieces

**This medieval recipe is spiced with cinnamon and cloves.
It has no tomatoes as in those days they they had not yet been
discovered. It is perfect served with the Pumpkin Gnocchi on
page 163 but is equally delicious served with Potato Gnocchi
(see page 156).**

Heat the oil in a large heavy-based saucepan and fry the leeks
gently over a low heat for around 10 minutes. Add the garlic and
continue to sweat for a further 5 minutes until the leeks are soft
and translucent. Add the lamb to the pan. Stir through then add
cloves, cinnamon and seasoning. Cook the lamb over a medium
heat for around 30 minutes, stirring frequently, until all the water
from the meat has evaporated and the lamb is dry. Make a
bouquet garni by bundling the herbs together in the middle of
a muslin cloth, close it up to make a bag and secure with string.
Add the wine, stock and bouquet garni to the pan and cook for
around 1 hour or until the sauce has reduced by half and the
lamb is soft. Taste and season further as necessary. Remove
the cinnamon stick and bouquet garni. Toss with gnocchi and
sprinkle with grated Parmesan.

POT ROAST GAME IN WINE

(Selvaggina in Umido)

SERVES 6

2 pheasants, 1 duck,
  4 partridges or 6 quails
fine salt and freshly
  ground black pepper
1–6 sprigs of thyme (1 per bird)
6 rashers (slices) unsmoked bacon
3 tablespoons extra-virgin olive oil
30 g (1 oz/2 tablespoons) salted butter
2 best quality Italian
  or pork sausages (optional)
1 white onion, roughly chopped
2 short sprigs of rosemary
1 bay leaf
200 ml (7 fl oz/scant 1 cup) white
  or madeira wine (or half and half)
100–200 ml (3½ –7 fl oz/
  scant ½ cup) Vegetable or
  Chicken stock (bouillon) or water

If you have ever roasted pheasant, partridge, rabbit, duck or quail and found it dry then you will know why I am more than happy to pot roast every time. Birds are not designed to be roasted, as their tough legs have higher collagen levels than their breasts so they need longer cooking. But if you get the legs right you have probably overcooked the breast and, conversely, if the breast is juicy the legs are pink and tough. The answer? Joint the bird and cook the pieces separately or pot roast slowly until the meat falls from the bones. Italian sausages have a great flavour as they contain garlic, wine and no bread. If you omit them add a couple of garlic cloves instead.

Preheat the oven to 160°C (320°F/Gas 3). Season the birds generously and wrap them in the bacon enclosing 1 sprig of thyme with each one. Secure with string or a toothpick. (If you find this challenging or are not going to serve the birds whole, simply cut the rashers into quarters and put them in the pot with the thyme.) Over the hob melt the butter and oil together in a flameproof casserole (one that has a lid) and brown the birds and sausages until golden all over. Add the onions, rosemary and bay leaf. When the onions have softened pour in the wine and let it bubble for a couple of minutes. Add the stock, put on the lid and transfer to the oven. Cook for the times stated opposite or until the meat falls from the bones easily.

Remove from the oven and check the level of liquid. Serve the birds straight away with the sauce (spoon off excess fat first) if you are happy with the taste and consistency. If you have a lot of liquid remove and rest the birds in a warm place covered with foil, then reduce the sauce over the heat on the hob, strain and serve. For a fatty bird like duck spoon away the oil first and reduce the sauce.

Pick all the meat from the bones and put it back into the pot with the sauce, heat through and stir into Potato Gnocchi (see page 156) or short pasta.

COOKING TIMES FOR THE BIRDS

Quails – around 1 hour
Partridges – 1½ hours
Pheasants – 1¾–2 hours
Duck – 2 hours

OXTAIL STEW

(Coda Alla Vaccinara)

Beef stew in all its forms is essential to the average Roman kitchen. It gives nourishment, comfort and that sense of security that comes from a ritual that you perform so regularly you can't imagine life without it. Even ragù, or meat sauce, that is made all over Italy is a form of stewed beef. Whether the meat is whole or ground, that marriage of beef and tomatoes cooked for a very long time together is hard to beat.

In Rome the Jewish have 'stracotto' meaning 'overcooked', born from a time when only the cheaper cuts were available to them. It was traditionally cooked on the ashes of a fire on a Friday so that it was still warm on the Sabbath when cooking was prohibited. It is a good idea to make this dish a day before you want to eat, allowing the fat to come to the surface overnight so that it can be removed.

Fill a large saucepan three quarters full with water and bring to the boil. Add the oxtail and bring the water back to the boil, then remove the oxtail from the water. Pour the water and any scum away. Boiling the oxtail like this will clean it and get rid of some of the fat.

Make the soffritto in a large saucepan; gently fry the vegetables in the olive oil with the seasoning and bay leaves for around 5–10 minutes over a medium heat until tender.

Heat the sunflower oil in a large frying pan over a medium–high heat and brown the oxtail all over. Transfer the oxtail to the soffritto and then pour over the wine. Allow it to reduce for a few minutes. Add the tomatoes, tomato purée and cinnamon. Wash the tomato tins out with a little water and add this to the tomatoes. Add enough stock to cover the oxtails. Turn down to simmer and cook, covered, for 5 hours or until the meat falls from the bones. During the cooking, turn the oxtails from time to time to make sure they don't stick and top up with a little stock or water, if necessary, so that they are always covered. You can also cook this in the oven: heat the oven to 160°C (320°F/Gas 4) and cook the stew in a casserole dish. Serve with mashed potato or Potato Gnocchi (see page 174).

SERVES 6

1.2 kg (2 lb 10 oz) oxtail
2 tablespoons sunflower oil
200 ml (7 oz) white wine
2 x 400 g (14 oz) tins
    plum tomatoes
1 heaped tablespoon
    tomato purée (paste)
1 small cinnamon stick
500 ml (17 fl oz) homemade
    meat or vegetable stock,
    as necessary

For the soffritto
6 celery sticks with leaves,
    coarsely chopped into
    5 mm (¼ in) cubes
2 medium white onions,
    coarsely chopped
2 carrots, coarsely chopped
8 tablespoons extra-virgin
    olive oil
3 teaspoons fine salt
½ teaspoon freshly
    ground black pepper
3 bay leaves

DUCK RAGÙ

(Sugo di 'Nana')

SERVES 6

5 tablespoons extra-virgin
  olive oil
4 large duck legs
  (about 1.5 kg/3 lb 5 oz)
salt and freshly ground
  black pepper
2 medium red onions,
  peeled and finely chopped
2 medium carrots,
  finely chopped
1 small celery stalk,
  finely chopped
4 bay leaves
200 g (7 oz) Fresh Tomato
  Passata (see page 73),
  or tinned tomatoes
300 ml (10 fl oz/1¼ cups)
  red wine
400–700 ml (13–24 fl oz/
  1¾–3 cups) chicken, meat or
  vegetable stock, or hot water

To serve
fresh pasta of choice
  (see page 26)
Ravioli stuffed with
  Potato & Cheese (see page 88)

Nana is Tuscan for 'duck', hence the Italian name for the sauce. Ducks are roasted, cooked in sauce or, in this case, used to make the famous Tuscan duck ragù. We use legs because they are cheaper than the breasts and have more flavour. You can use the whole duck, jointed, but since you have to pick the meat from the bones it is easier to do this with the legs. This type of sauce is typically served with fresh pasta such as tagliatelle or maltagliati – the misshapen pieces – or the potato-filled *Ravioli di Mugello* (see page 88), and is not normally served with cheese.

Heat the oil in a large non-stick frying pan over a high heat until hot, then lay the duck legs skin side down in the pan. Season generously. Leave to brown for about 10 minutes or until the skin is golden and crisp, then turn them over to brown on the other side. Now, season this side of the legs. Reduce the heat to medium and add the chopped onions, carrots, celery and the bay leaves. Stir through then tuck the bay leaves under the duck. Cook for around 10 minutes, stirring occasionally.

Meanwhile blend the tinned tomatoes (if using instead of passata) in a food processor or push them through a sieve into a bowl. Add the wine to the duck pan and allow it to bubble and evaporate for a few minutes, and for the strong smell of alcohol to diminish, then add the tomatoes and 400 ml (13 fl oz/1¾ cups) of the stock or water. Bring to the boil, remove the bay leaves and taste the sauce. Add seasoning to taste and loosely cover the pan with a lid. Leave to cook over a low heat for around 1 hour or until the meat falls off the bones easily (push a knife into the meat to see how soft it is). You may need to add the remaining stock if it reduces too much. Remove the pan from the heat and leave to cool. When the legs are cool enough to touch, remove them from the pan and pull off the meat and skin. Discard the bones and skin. Roughly chop the meat then put it back into the pan and stir. If eating straight away, heat and mix with cooked pasta in the pan and serve. Or, chill and keep in the fridge for up to 4 days, or freeze for up to 3 months.

SAUSAGE, PORCINI & BACON SAUCE FOR SCIALATIELLI

(Sugo di Salsiccia Porcini and Pancetta)

Scialatielli are a pasta specialty of the Amalfi coast and are made with either basil for meat sauces or parsley for fish. These robust and flavourful ribbons are good enough to eat on their own but here they are served with a sausage meat sauce. Italians split open garlicky sausages with a good fat content and no rusk and crumble the meat into the pan. If you can't find them us a good pork mince instead.

Heat the oil in a large frying pan. Cut open the sausages and remove the meat. Crumble the sausage meat into the pan and break it up with a wooden spoon. Add the porcini, pancetta or bacon and garlic to the pan, and fry until the meat is lightly browned and cooked through. Add the cherry tomatoes and briefly cook until just soft. Cook the scialatielli and combine with the sauce before serving.

SERVES 4
(as a main, 6 as a starter)

2 tablespoons extra-virgin
 olive oil
200 g (7 oz) Italian sausages
50 g (2 oz) dried porcini,
 soaked and sliced
50 g (2 oz) smoked pancetta
 or smoked bacon, cut into strips
2 garlic cloves, lightly crushed
10 cherry tomatoes, quartered
1 quantity of Scialatielli
 (see page 34), to serve

CANNELLONI

SERVES 4–6

The trick with cannelloni, as far as I am concerned, is to think about the dish you're going to serve it in and try to plan out how to cut and fill the pasta. Pasta swells by 30 per cent when cooked so you'll need to cut your pasta according to the size of the dish. I have given instructions for my lasagna dish but you could just as well cut the pasta sheets in half and make more small rolls. Cannelloni freezes well so I often double the recipe quantities and make two trays. The ragù uses strong-flavoured Italian sausages with no added rusk. If you can't find them, use diced salami or an end of leg of prosciutto (all of these are usually available from Italian delis).

First, make the ragù. Heat the oil in a pan and fry the vegetables with the garlic, bay leaves and rosemary for about 15 minutes, or until soft. Add the meats and brown them well. Allow any meat juices to evaporate before adding the wine and tomato purée. Cook the ragù for about 1 hour over a low heat, adding a little water if the sauce looks dry. Taste and add seasoning if necessary. Remove the pan from the heat and leave the sauce to cool. Transfer to a bowl, stir in the ricotta and refrigerate.

Meanwhile, make the pasta following the instructions on page 26. Roll the dough through a pasta machine so that its width spans the machine, which is usually about 14 cm (5½ in). Put it through twice on the stop before last on the machine so that it is neither too thick nor too thin that it will fall apart. (The last setting makes the thinnest pasta but this is too fragile for cannelloni.) Cut the pasta into 11 cm (4¼ in) lengths. You should end up with around 10–12 rectangles of pasta measuring 14 x 11 cm (5½ x 4¼ in) and some offcuts.

Bring a large pan of well-salted water to the boil. Fill a large bowl with cold water and spread out 2 clean tea towels on your work surface. Cook the pasta for 2–3 minutes until al dente, then carefully remove the sheets with tongs and put into the cold water. As soon as they are cool enough to handle, lay them out on the tea towels to drain.

For the ragù

100 ml (3½ fl oz/½ cup) extra-virgin olive oil
1 large carrot, finely diced
2 celery stalks, finely diced
1 red onion, peeled and finely diced
1 garlic clove, lightly crushed
2 bay leaves
1 sprig of rosemary
300 g (10½ oz) coarse (not extra lean) minced beef
200 g (7 oz) Italian sausages, salami or prosciutto end
200 ml (7 fl oz/scant 1 cup) red wine
2 tablespoons tomato purée
salt and freshly ground black pepper
2 tablespoons ricotta

To serve

basil oil or olive oil for drizzling (optional)
shavings of Parmesan or Grana Padano
a few basil leaves, to garnish

Preheat the oven to 180°C (350°F/Gas 4). Pour one-third of the tomato sauce into a lasagne dish measuring about 20 x 35 cm (8 x 14 in). To make up the cannelloni, put 3 tablespoons of the ragù along one long edge of a sheet of pasta. Roll it up like a cigar and lay it in the lasagne dish. Repeat with the remaining sheets until the ragù is used up. (Any leftover pasta sheets can be oiled then frozen flat in a stack and used another day.) Pour over enough of the remaining tomato sauce to cover the cannelloni and drizzle over a little basil oil or olive oil, if liked. (Again, any leftover tomato sauce can be kept for a pasta sauce for another day.)

Bake for 25 minutes or until bubbling hot throughout. Either sprinkle the shaved Parmesan or Grana Padano over halfway through cooking time or when serving. Serve with basil leaves to garnish.

RITA'S RAVIOLI

(Ravioli di Rita)

Rita is from Vicenza, a small town not far from Venice. She lives in the UK now but still cooks *alla vicentina* and she makes the most wonderful *ravioli in brodo* for her family at Christmas. Luckily I know her daughter-in-law so once a year I eat her ravioli in chicken broth. Like a mother's hug, this food is about as comforting as you can get. This recipe makes a lot of pasta but it does freeze well, so we make enough to eat straight away and freeze the rest for another day. The chicken stock (bouillon) is best homemade and flavoured with Parmesan rinds, which gives it a moreish, umami hit.

Melt the butter in a frying pan over a medium heat then add the onion. After a few minutes add the garlic and continue to gently fry until the onion softens. Don't let it burn. Add the minced meats and brown, stirring frequently. Pour in the wine. Cover, reduce the heat and cook gently for around 20 minutes, keeping an eye on it so that it doesn't catch. When the meat is very tender, carefully pour the mixture into a food processor and blend into a smooth paste. Transfer the blended meat to a mixing bowl and stir in the parsley, breadcrumbs, Parmesan and egg yolk. Combine well and season to taste.

Roll out the pasta using a pasta maker set on the thinnest setting. Line a ravioli tray with a sheet of the pasta. Spoon a fat pea-size ball of filling into each indent and place another sheet of pasta over the top. With a rolling pin, roll the pasta to ensure that the 2 layers are sealed together. If the pasta has dried out a little while you were dividing out the stuffing, brush with a little water before laying over the top sheet to ensure a good seal. Turn out on to greaseproof (wax) paper and repeat. The ravioli can be made in advance and frozen.

If you are using homemade stock, leave the Parmesan rinds in. If using shop-bought stock, add 3 Parmesan rinds to it to give it the depth of flavor. Bring the chicken stock to a simmer in a large saucepan and season to taste. Add the ravioli and cook for around 12–14 minutes. This pasta is usually eaten soft rather than al dente. Serve with love and grated Parmesan.

SERVES 12
(makes around 80–90 ravioli)

2 quantities of fresh pasta
    (see page 26)
3 litres fresh or bought
    chicken stock (bouillon)

For the filling
 50 g (2 oz/½ stick) salted butter
½ onion or 1 small shallot,
    finely chopped
2 garlic cloves, finely chopped
100 g (3½ oz) minced (ground)
    veal or chicken or turkey
100 g (3½ oz) minced pork
4 tablespoons white wine
handful of parsley,
    finely chopped
60 g (2 oz/¾ cup)
    fresh breadcrumbs
50 g (2 oz) Parmesan, finely
    grated, plus more to serve
1 egg yolk
freshly ground black pepper
    and sea salt

PASTA TUBES WITH SWEET ONION & BEEF SAUCE

(Paccheri all Genovese)

The savoury but sweet combination of slow-cooked onions and beef is heavenly. This sauce is cooked for a whole day to achieve a deep, rich flavour. It can be made using tuna instead of beef, in which case the cooking time is reduced to 3 hours. The Genovese sauce is always served with paccheri – large tubes – of pasta.

Start by making the sauce. Put all the ingredients excluding the milk and wine into a large saucepan. Bring to the boil and then turn down the heat. Cover and simmer for 7–8 hours. After 1½ hours of cooking time stir in the milk. After another 1½ hours, stir in the wine. Check every now and again to see if the sauce looks dry; if it does, add a little more water. At the end of the cooking time, taste the sauce – it should be soft and sweet. Serve with onion rings dipped in flour and deep-fried until crisp.

SERVES 10–12

For the sauce
2 kg (4½ lb) red onions, peeled and finely sliced into half rings
750 g (1lb 1oz) stewing steak (chuck steak)
200 ml (7 fl oz/scant 1 cup) extra-virgin olive oil
200 g (7 oz) carrots coarsely grated salt and freshly ground black pepper
200 ml (7 fl oz/scant 1 cup) water
175 ml (6 fl oz/¾ cup) milk
250 ml (8½ fl oz/1 cup) white wine

To serve
1 white onion, sliced into rings
flour, for coating
sunflower oil, for frying

PASTA WITH SAUSAGE RAGÙ & KALE

(Fusilli con Salsiccia Ragù e Cavola Nero)

If you can, find Italian sausages to give this sauce a more genuine Tuscan taste; however, we frequently make it with good-quality English ones, as long as the meat is coarsely ground and they are not stuffed with rusk. Italian sausages are made with 100 per cent meat, have a good fat content and are flavoured with salt and garlic, and are often used in Italian recipes as sausage meat or instead of minced meat. If you do find them you may not need any extra garlic or salt in the recipe. This recipe comes from Raffaella Cecchelli who runs the smallest osteria in Italy called La Tana dei Brillo Parlante in the stunningly pretty town of Massa Marittima. In the photo we have used fresh pappardelle, but this sauce is also ideal with penne, fusilli or rigatoni dried pasta.

Bring a large saucepan of salted water to the boil, add the cavolo nero and cook for 5–10 minutes until soft. Drain well and set aside. When cool enough to touch, cut the leaves into shreds.

Make a shallow incision along the length of the sausages with a knife and peel away the skin. Discard the skins and crumble the meat into a large frying pan, then add the oil, garlic and chilli. Put the pan over a medium heat and cook until the sausage meat is lightly browned, breaking it up with a wooden spoon as it cooks.

Meanwhile, cook the pasta according to the packet instructions (see page 19) and time it so the pasta will be just cooked when the sauce is ready.

Add the white wine to the sausage mixture in the frying pan and allow this to evaporate for around 5 minutes, then add the shredded cavolo nero and stir through. Pour in the cream, if using, bring the sauce to a gentle boil and taste for seasoning (sometimes there is no need add more salt if the sausages are already salty). Stir hot, drained pasta into the sauce and serve straight away with the grated Parmesan.

SERVES 6

300 g (10½ oz) cavolo nero
(or other cabbage), washed,
tough stems removed and leaves
roughly chopped
6 good-quality (over 90% meat)
pork sausages
5 tablespoons extra-virgin olive oil
2 fat garlic cloves, peeled and
lightly crushed
fresh red chilli, sliced, to taste,
or ¼ teaspoon dried chilli flakes
480 g (17 oz) dried pasta
3 tablespoons white wine
100 ml (3½ fl oz/scant ½ cup)
double (heavy) cream (optional)
salt and freshly ground black pepper
25 g (1 oz) grated Parmesan

PASTA WITH TOMATO, BACON & ONION SAUCE

(Rigatoni I All'Amatriciana)

SERVES 6

5 tablespoons extra-virgin
  olive oil
500 g (1 lb 2 oz) white onion,
  finely sliced into semi-circles
250 g (9 oz) guanciale,
  pancetta or streaky bacon,
  cut into 5 mm (¼ in) strips
salt and freshly ground
  black pepper
100 ml (3½ fl oz) white wine
2 x 400 g (14 oz) tins good-quality
  plum tomatoes, crushed
  with your hands
500 g (1 lb 2 oz) rigatoni
50 g (2 oz) Pecorino Romano
  or Parmesan, finely grated

Traditionally this sauce is served with bucatini, as in the photo. It is one of the silliest forms of pasta ever made. It is thick and difficult to wrap around your fork, whips around your face as you suck it in and whistles as the air passes through it almost so as to draw attention to your lack of finesse. It also splashes its bright red coating of sauce around your face and clothes. No thank you. Give me good old rigatoni or penne any day. However, a well-made *amatriciana* sauce is something to write home about. *Guanciale*, or cured pig's cheeks, is the background meaty flavour imparted by the layers of fat and meat in a cheek that has been coated in pepper and hung in a curing cabinet for months. This renders the *guanciale* sweet, firm to slice and with a kick of umami that is not delivered by the modern slice of mass-produced bacon. If you can't find this, or indeed proper pancetta, buy the best unsmoked streaky, fatty bacon you can find.

'Amatriciana' comes from Amatrice, a town in the mountainous region of Lazio. This area was Abruzzo before Mussolini changed the border lines. Apparently, this dish originally derives from the mountain people who lived there, who called it la gricia, which in those days was simply fried *guanciale*, pasta, black pepper and pecorino, sometimes with a dash of vinegar. Tomatoes were a later addition by the wealthier people of the area who could afford them, and it then became known as *amatriciana*.

Heat the oil in a large frying pan and fry the onion, guanciale, salt and pepper for around 10 minutes until the onion has softened. Add the wine and allow to reduce for about 5 minutes, then add the crushed tomatoes and cook over a gentle simmer for 30 minutes until the sauce reduces and thickens. About 10 minutes before you are ready to serve, cook the pasta in a large pan of salted boiling water according to the packet instructions until al dente. Adjust the seasoning in the sauce as necessary and serve tossed with the drained hot pasta and cheese.

KALE & RICOTTA GNOCCHI IN SAGE & BACON BUTTER

(Gnocchi Nudi in Salsa di Burro, Salvia e Pancetta)

SERVES 4
(as a main, 6 as a starter –
makes approximately 36 gnocchi)

For the gnocchi
300 g (10½ oz) fresh curly kale
 or cavolo nero, or 200 g (7 oz)
 cooked and thoroughly squeezed
 curly kale or cavolo nero leaves
250 g (9 oz/1 cup) ricotta, drained
100 g (3½ oz) grated Parmesan
 or Pecorino
1 egg
3 heaped tablespoons wheat
 or gluten-free flour, plus extra
 for dusting
¼ teaspoon finely grated nutmeg
1 teaspoon salt, plus extra for
 the cooking water
freshly ground black pepper
25 g (1 oz) grated Parmesan,
 plus extra, to serve

For the bacon, butter and
 sage sauce
100 g (3½ oz) unsalted butter
150 g (5 oz) unsmoked or smoked
 pancetta or bacon, cut into
 small strips
10 sage leaves
salt, to taste
freshly ground black pepper
 (optional)
30 g (1 oz) pine nuts,
 toasted (optional)

In Florence, the name of these gnocchi literally means 'nude' gnocchi as they are like the spinach and ricotta stuffing that you find in ravioli only without their pasta clothes. If you don't have kale, use spinach or Swiss chard leaves instead. Serve them with the bacon, butter and sage sauce or Our Favourite Tomato Sauce on page 72.

Start by making the gnocchi. If using fresh kale or cavolo nero, pull away the tough stems. Roughly cut the leaves and boil them in salted water for 10 minutes. Drain well and set aside.

When cool enough to handle, thoroughly squeeze out the excess water from the kale (to the last drop!) and finely chop in a food processor (or by hand with a sharp knife on a board), then put into a bowl. Add the remaining ingredients for the gnocchi to the kale and stir through to combine. The mixture should be firm enough to handle and not wet and sticky. If it is too sticky, add a little more flour to the mix.

Roll the mixture into walnut-sized balls, making sure they are tightly packed so that they don't break up in the water. As you prepare the balls, put them on a floured surface. You can keep them like this in the fridge, loosely covered, for up to a day if you want to prepare them in advance.

Prepare the sauce by melting the butter in a large frying pan. Add the bacon, sage leaves, salt and pepper (if using) and fry until the bacon is cooked through and the sage leaves are lightly browned. Add a ladleful of hot water and stir well. Leave the sauce over a very low heat while you cook the gnocchi.

Bring a large pan of well salted water to the boil. Turn the heat down to medium – unlike when cooking pasta, you want a slow rolling boil, not a rapid boil. Drop the gnocchi carefully into the water. Let the water come back up to the boil and cook for 3–4 minutes until the gnocchi rise up to the surface. Let them bob around for a further minute, then remove them from the water with a slotted spoon and lower them into the butter sauce. Fry them in the sauce for a few minutes until lightly browned. Stir the pine nuts in, if using. Serve with extra grated Parmesan on top.

LITTLE MEAT PATTIES

(Polpettine di Carne)

These meatballs are typical of the Amalfi coast region. They are given an almost Arabic twist with the addition of sultanas and pine nuts, which enhance both taste and texture. The recipe works equally well without them, so leave them out if you wish.

Soak the sultanas in warm water (if using) and the bread in milk for 10 minutes while you prepare the rest of the ingredients. Finely chop the parsley and garlic together, using a large knife. Transfer to a bowl with the meat, seasoning, eggs, pine nuts (if using) and grated cheese. Drain the sultanas and add these to the bowl (if using). Squeeze the bread and discard the milk, then break it up into very small pieces and add it to the bowl. Use your hands to mix the ingredients together.

Wet your hands and shape the mixture into meatballs the shape of rugby balls measuring approximately 7 x 4 cm (2¾ x 1½ in). Lay them on a tray while you complete the task.

Heat the oil in a large frying pan. Coat the meatballs in flour and tap off the excess. Fry the balls in batches in the hot oil until lightly browned all over. They will cook further in the tomato sauce, so do not worry about them not being cooked through. Once browned, remove them from the pan with a slotted spoon and drain on kitchen paper.

Discard the oil from the pan and make the tomato sauce, following the recipe on page 72. Add the meatballs to the sauce and cook for about 30 minutes over a low to medium heat until the meat is cooked through (test by cutting into a meatball: the inside should be brown and not red). The Italians would eat this with the bread, followed by a salad afterwards.

SERVES 6
(makes around 20–24 patties)

75 g (2½ oz/generous ½ cup) sultanas (optional)
200 g (7 oz) stale white rustic bread, crusts removed
500 ml (17 fl oz/generous 2 cups full-fat milk
small handful of parsley
1 small garlic cloves
500 g (1 lb 2 oz/2 cups) lean minced (ground) beef, or half beef and half pork
salt and freshly ground black pepper
2 eggs
40 g (1½ oz/¼ cup) pine nuts (optional)
100 g (3½ oz) Grana Padano, finely grated
5 tablespoons sunflower oil
'00' or plain (all-purpose) flour, to coat the patties
1 quantity of Our Favourite Tomato Sauce (see page 72)

PASTA WITH BROCCOLI & SAUSAGE RAGÙ

(Pasta con Broccoli e Ragù di Salsiccia)

SERVES 4
(as a main, or 6 as a starter)

Italian delis sell sausages that are perfect for this dish as they are made of pure pork and have no bread or rusk content. If you can't find them look for coarse-grained pork sausages that contain little or no wheat. In winter sauteed mushrooms are a good substitute for broccoli. Giancarlo stirs a couple of tablespoons of cream into the finished sauce to bind it together, though this isn't strictly necessary. This sauce is also eaten on its own without the pasta: in Praiano it is eaten in a sandwich and drunk with red wine for the feast of San Martino.

3 tablespoons extra-virgin olive oil
1 onion, finely chopped
1 large garlic clove, finely chopped
salt and freshly ground black pepper
½ red chilli, finely chopped
250 g (9 oz) broccoli florets
400 g (14 oz) Italian sausages
75 ml (2 fl oz/⅓ cup) white wine
250 g (9 oz) orecchiette or
*   short pasta such as penne*
25 g (1 oz) Parmesan or
*   Grana Padano, finely grated*
best quality extra-virgin olive oil,
*   for drizzling*

Bring a large pan of well-salted water to the boil and add the pasta. Heat the oil in a large non-stick frying pan and fry the onion over a medium heat for 5–7 minutes until softened. Add the garlic, black pepper and chilli and cook for a further couple of minutes, being careful not to burn the garlic. Only add salt later if necessary, as sausages are often salty.

Meanwhile, steam or briefly boil the broccoli florets until just cooked. Cut open the sausages and remove the meat. Crumble the sausage meat into the pan and break it up with a wooden spoon. Cook until browned, then pour in the wine and allow it to reduce for a few minutes. Keep the sauce over a low heat while you cook the pasta. When the pasta is al dente, drain and add the broccoli. Add the pasta and broccoli to the frying pan, along with a tablespoon of cooking water to lengthen the sauce. Stir through gently, taste and adjust the seasoning if necessary. Serve in warmed bowls with a scattering of Parmesan or Grana Padano, a twist of black pepper and a drizzle of your best olive oil.

FISH/ SEAFOOD

In my hometown of Eastbourne, there is a fresh fish shop called Southern Head Fishing Company. I love to go there when we visit the town and select the freshest mackerel, lobster, mussels and cuttlefish straight from the local boats; it reminds me of the wonderful market stalls in Italy where raucous fisherman ply their trade. Every coastal town in Italy has recipes for fish soups, sauces and seafood pastas. We might not have exactly the same species back home but with some substitutions we can achieve the same results. I think people are scared of cooking seafood, but actually with a little practice it is a quick, delicious and healthy source of nutrition.

ROMANESCO WITH PASTA

(Pasta con Broccolo Romanesco in Tegame)

SERVES 4

500 g (1 lb 2 oz) Romanesco
   or white cauliflower
4 tablespoons extra-virgin olive oil
1 onion, finely chopped
3 anchovy fillets in oil, drained
1 bay leaf
1 tablespoon currants
   or small raisins
1 tablespoon pine nuts
pinch of saffron strands
salt and freshly ground
   black pepper
handful of dry breadcrumbs
   or finely grated Parmesan,
   to serve (optional)

Broccolo here refers to those green pointed Romanesco cauliflowers that look like an incredible, miniature work of architecture. You can, however, make this sauce with white cauliflower – both types soften down to create a creamy pasta sauce. At Mandranova *agriturismo* near Agrigento, Silvia Di Vincenzo stirred the cauliflower into pasta shells. The shapes caught the soft florets with the *pinoli* (pine nuts) and tiny black currants. Local *pinoli* are long, fruity and oily, and have a distinct flavour a world apart from the tiny dry Chinese imported ones. Seek them out if you can. This is supposed to be a sauce for pasta but for me it also makes the most delicious soupy stew to eat on a cold autumn day. To add a little crunch, you can top the dish with toasted breadcrumbs and a little grated hard cheese. Cooking the pasta in the *broccolo* water enhances the flavour, too.

Cut the Romanesco or cauliflower into florets and discard the leaves (you can use these too if you have lots of them). Plunge them into salted boiling water and cook until just tender when pierced with a fork. Get a large bowl of iced water ready. Remove the florets with a slotted spoon and drop them into the chilled water to cool and to keep their colour. Retain the cooking water.

Drain the Romanesco and use your hands to break the florets into smaller pieces. Heat the oil in a frying pan (skillet) and fry the onion and anchovies until just softened. Add the Romanesco, bay leaf, currants and pine nuts, then top up with the Romanesco cooking water to cover. Soften the saffron strands in a tablespoon of hot water and stir into the pan. Break up the Romanesco with a wooden spoon so that the sauce becomes dense and creamy. Taste and adjust the seasoning as necessary. Eat as it is or with cooked dried pasta, sprinkled with breadcrumbs or Parmesan, if you like.

PASTA WITH SARDINES & ONIONS

(Bigoli in Salsa)

This is an unbelievably tasty dish made from just three main ingredients. The softened onions and fish form a creamy sauce to coat the pasta, which is incredibly moreish. This dish was typically eaten in Venetian households on Fridays during Lent, as in the past meat was banned. It is popular at all times now and also forms part of a grand fish feast on Christmas Eve in many homes. Use anchovies if you can't find sardines.

A note on Parmesan: I have made Venetians gasp in horror as they rarely put fish and cheese together but a sprinkling of finely grated Parmesan is gorgeous on this dish.

Heat the oil in a large saucepan, add the onions and bay leaf, if using, and turn the heat to low. Cook slowly for around 15 minutes until soft, shaking and stirring the pan frequently with a wooden spoon. Rinse the fish in cold water if they are in salt; if they are in oil don't worry. Bring to the boil a large pot of well-salted water, add the pasta and cook for 8–10 minutes or until al dente. Meanwhile, put the sardines in with the onions and break up the fish with a wooden spoon until they blend with the onions. Add the white wine to the fish and onions and allow the alcohol to evaporate for a couple of minutes. Season with pepper and taste, only add salt if necessary. Take a couple of ladlefuls of the water from the pot of pasta and reserve in a jug. Drain the pasta and add to the fish mixture with a little of the cooking water as necessary to create a sauce. Toss through and serve with a sprinkling of parsley if using.

SERVES 4
(as a main, 6 as a starter)

4 tablespoons extra-virgin olive oil
2 large brown onions, finely chopped
1 small bay leaf (optional)
360 g (12½ oz) bigoli or spaghetti
240 g (8½ oz) tinned salted sardines
    or 60 g tinned anchovy fillets,
    net weight, in salt or oil
4 tablespoons white wine
salt and freshly ground black pepper
handful of parsley, finely chopped,
    to serve (optional)

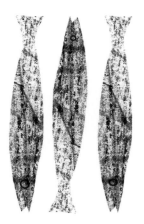

PRAWN STOCK

Any time we use shellfish such as crabs, prawns (shrimp), crayfish, langoustines and lobsters we buy them with their heads and shells so that we can keep them for making a stock. This broth adds a wonderful flavour to any seafood dish and no shop-bought stock compares to it.

Heat the oil in a large stock pot over a medium heat. Add the shells and heads with the carrot and onion. When the shells start to brown and stick to the bottom of the pan add the wine, increase the heat and let it reduce for 4–5 minutes. Bash the shells, particularly any prawn or lobster heads, with a wooden rolling pin to release the juices and break up the shells. Pour in the hot water, bring to the boil, then reduce the heat and simmer for 1–1½ hours. We don't skim this broth as you lose the flavour and orange colour that way. Remove from the heat. Strain the stock into a large jug or bowl, squeezing the juices from the shells by pressing down on them with a ladle. Discard the shells. Use the stock straight away or store in an airtight container in the fridge for up to 4 days. You can also simmer the stock for a further 45 minutes to reduce it and then pour into ice cube trays or small bags and freeze for up to 3 months.

**Makes approx. 2 litres
(3½ pints/8½ cups)**

3 tablespoons extra-virgin olive oil
1.5 kg (3 lb 5 oz) raw seafood
    shells and heads
1 medium carrot, halved lengthways,
    or large handful of carrot peelings
1 white onion, roughly chopped,
    or large handful of onion peelings
100 ml (3½ fl oz/scant ½ cup)
    white wine
3 litres (5¼ pints/12¾ cups) hot water

SARDINE & WILD FENNEL SAUCE

(Pasta con Le Sarde e Finocchio Selvatici)

Pasta con *le sarde* is almost a national dish in Sicily and is found in various forms all over the island. It is indeed a recipe that serves up a rich, splendid plate of history, showing Arab and Italian traditions together. The typical pasta to eat with it is busiate, twirls of pasta made from semolina flour (see page 27) but spaghetti is a good substitute. This recipe is from passionate foodie Caterina, owner of Il Palladio hotel and restaurant in Giardini Naxos. She uses abundant handfuls of wild fennel and local sardines. In the UK, wild fennel grows both in gardens and in the countryside, so do seek it out. If you can't find it, use fresh dill instead. If you can get hold of the long, Italian pine nuts, they add flavor as well as crunch to the pasta. They are expensive but if you are travelling in Sicily they are widely available at the markets.

Fry the onion, garlic and chilli together in the oil until soft. Boil the wild fennel whole for 5 minutes and save the water to cook your pasta later. Squeeze the fennel to get rid of the excess water and chop finely. Melt the anchovies in the oil with the onion and add the pine nuts, raisins, fennel and tomatoes. Season to taste. Add the sardines and the saffron mixed with 2 tablespoons of hot water, cover and leave to cook for 5 minutes or until the fish is cooked through. Break the fish up a little and taste the sauce. Season as necessary. Boil the reserved fennel water in a large pan and add the spaghetti. Cook until tender according to the manufacturer's suggestions and drain. Add just-cooked pasta to the sauce and toss to combine. Serve in warm bowls topped with the almonds.

SERVES 4
(as a main, 6 as a starter)

1 white onion, finely chopped
1 garlic clove, peeled and
   roughly chopped
a little fresh red chilli or a
   pinch of dried chilli flakes,
   to taste
6 tablespoons extra-virgin
   olive oil
large handful of wild fennel
5 anchovies in oil, drained
1 heaped tablespoon pine nuts
2 tablespoons soft,
   sweet raisins or currants
handful of cherry tomatoes,
   roughly chopped
salt and freshly ground
   black pepper
10 fresh sardines, filleted
good pinch of saffron strands
320 g (11 oz) spaghetti
handful of toasted flaked
   almonds, roughly crushed

SPAGHETTI WITH ANCHOVIES, CAPERS & CHERRY TOMATOES

(Spaghetti di Grano Duro con Capperi di Pantelleria e Pomodorino di Pachino)

SERVES 4
(as a main, 6 as a starter)

1 onion, finely chopped
25 g (1 oz) anchovy fillets,
    fresh or tinned in oil, drained
2 tablespoons extra-virgin olive oil
400 g (14 oz) cherry tomatoes,
    cut into quarters
handful of olives, pitted
3 tablespoons small capers
    in salt, well rinsed
salt and freshly ground
    black pepper
320 g (11½ oz) durum
    wheat spaghetti
a little strong extra-virgin
    olive oil, to serve
3 tablespoons finely chopped
    parsley, to garnish
a handful of olives, pitted

This quick-to-cook pasta dish appears in various guises all over the island. It is made from ingredients that you normally have to hand and never fails to please. This recipe is from Stefano Gegnacorsi, the hard-working general manager of the Belmond Grand Hotel Timeo in Taormina. He told us that after a busy day at the hotel this is what he goes home to cook. Try to find small capers sold in salt and give them a good rinse – the best ones come from the sunny island of Pantelleria.

Prepare the sauce by sautéing the onion with the anchovies in a little of their oil and the olive oil over a low heat for up to 10 minutes or until softened, but make sure they don't take on any colour. Add the cherry tomatoes, olives and capers to the pan and season to taste. You may not need any salt as the anchovies are already salty.

Put the pasta on to cook in a large saucepan of boiling salted water. Cook until tender, according to the packet instructions.

Add the just-cooked and drained pasta to the sauce and toss, allowing a little of the pasta water to fall into the pan – this will help to dilute and emulsify the sauce. Finish with a swirl of your best peppery extra-virgin olive oil, a scattering of parsley and the olives. Serve in warm bowls.

GIANFRANCO'S RICOTTA GNOCCHI 'NDUNDERI

SERVES 4
(as a main course or 6 as a starter – makes 30 gnocchi)

350 g (12 oz) ricotta
150 g (5 oz/1¼ cups) '00' flour
35 g (1¼ oz) Parmesan,
* finely grated*
1 teaspoon salt
pinch of white pepper
* (optional)*

For the sauce
5 tablespoons extra-virgin
* olive oil*
1 courgette (zucchini),
* cut into fine strips*
600 g (1lb 5 oz) clams
1 large garlic clove, lightly crushed
freshly ground black pepper
50 ml (2 fl oz/¼ cup) white wine
handful of parsley,
* roughly chopped*

To serve
shavings of pecorino (optional)

These beautifully light ricotta gnocchi are the speciality of Minori. We visited the restaurant Il Giardiniello, where they are made by the owner's mother, to sample them. Here they are served in a rich tomato sauce softened by the smoky provola cheese. Our friend Gianfranco from the Amalfi Coast makes them at his restaurant Zero in Hertfordshire and this is his recipe – minus the eggs – to keep them light. Usually cheese is not served with shellfish, but on the Amalfi Coast they make an exception and I simply love it.

Start by making the gnocchi. Mix the ingredients together in a bowl and knead for a couple of minutes only on a floured work surface. Gianfranco's tip is that the less you work the dough, the better. Roll the dough into long, fat sausages and cut into smaller 4 cm (1½ inch) lengths. Use a ridged board or the side of a grater to roll them into large curls, using three fingertips to push them down. Repeat until the dough is finished and set aside on a floured surface.

Bring a large pan of well-salted water to the boil. Meanwhile, prepare the sauce. Heat 1 tablespoon of oil in a large frying pan and fry the courgette strips until crispy. Remove from the pan and set aside on kitchen paper to drain. Heat the remaining oil in the pan and when hot add the clams and garlic, then cover. Shake the pan frequently and cook until all the clams have opened. Discard any that do not open. Pour in the wine and allow the sauce to reduce slightly.

Meanwhile, cook the gnocchi. Drop them into the boiling water and cook for about 3 minutes. They will float to the surface when cooked. Lift them out gently, using a slotted spoon, and toss them into the pan with the clams, along with a tablespoon of cooking water. Add the parsley, and serve in warmed bowls with the shavings of Pecorino.

SPAGHETTI WITH PRAWNS & TOMATO

(Spaghetti e Scampi alla Busara all'Ada)

500 g (1 lb 2 oz) raw prawns
    (shrimp), shells and heads
    on if possible
salt and freshly ground
    black pepper
50 g (2 oz/½ cup) '00'
    or plain (all-purpose) flour
2 garlic cloves, whole,
    peeled and lightly crushed
5 tablespoons extra-virgin olive oil
2 tablespoons cognac
400 g (14 oz/1½ cups) tomato
    passata or tinned Italian
    whole plum tomatoes puréed
    in a blender
1 tablespoon tomato purée
    (tomato paste)
½ –1 red fresh or dried chilli,
    finely chopped, to taste, or
    2 tablespoons ground hot paprika
350 g (12 oz) spaghetti
handful of parsley, finely chopped,
    to serve

The wonderful chef Ada Catto worked at Ca' D'Oro – known locally as Alla Vedova, meaning the Widow's Place – for 30 years where this dish was served in multitude every day. Ada uses chilli to give it a kick of spice, and other Venetians have told me they use paprika to give it a sweet spicy flavour. I make this dish spicy so if you prefer it milder then reduce the amount of chilli to suit your taste. Do taste the chilli before adding it to the dish as they vary in strength. Ada also recommended using good homemade tomato passata, but failing that use Italian tinned tomatoes and tomato purée (tomato paste). If you can find them use prawns with their heads still on, as that is where the flavour lies. If you can't find them, to get a stronger flavour of shellfish add 100 ml (3½ fl oz/scant ½ cup) of seafood stock (bouillon) with the tomatoes.

Remove the shells and tails from the prawns leaving the heads attached to the body. Make a shallow cut down the length of the back of the body and remove the black vein. Put them into a mixing bowl and season, then add the flour and toss with your hands to coat the prawns. Fry the garlic in a large frying pan in the oil for 1 minute over a medium heat. Take the prawns from the flour, shaking off any excess, and add to the pan. Very briefly fry the prawns until they are pink and the flour has slightly browned. Add the cognac, shake the pan and when the strong smell of alcohol has dissipated remove them from the pan with a slotted spoon. Set aside in a bowl. Leave the garlic in the pan and add the chilli, fry for 1 minute. Add the tomatoes and tomato purée, and leave it to cook, stirring every now and again, for 15–20 minutes over a low heat so it is just bubbling.

Bring a large pot of salted water to the boil and cook the spaghetti for 8–10 minutes or until al dente. Halfway through put the prawns into the tomato sauce along with any juices in the bowl. Taste the sauce and season as necessary. Drain the pasta and add to the tomato sauce and toss or stir through the sauce. Divide among 4 warm bowls and scatter over the parsley to serve.

FISH SAUCE

(Ragù de Pesce)

Use a mixture of fish, as each one will impart its own flavour. In Palermo there was a fishmonger who had a large marble slab covered in tiny or broken fish, the kind of scraps that would be perfect for this dish. By 10:30 am the slab was cleared and the Sicilians were on their way home with bags of cheap fish for a tasty ragù. Do make the prawn stock on page 141 – I freeze it into ice cube trays and pop a cube or two into any fish sauce to increase the flavour. Since we don't have a fishmonger near our home, I put a few shell-on prawns (shrimp) into the sauce to give it a stronger flavour. This sauce is best with dried pasta such as spaghetti.

Heat the oil in a large saucepan and fry the shallot, carrot, celery and garlic with the bay leaf and parsley stalks over a low heat for 5 minutes. Peel the prawns and discard the shells. Remove the heads and set aside. Add the tomatoes, chilli and prawn heads, if using, followed by the stock, to the pan and bring to the boil. Let it cook slowly for 10 minutes. Use tongs to fish out the prawn heads and squeeze the juices out into the pan. Discard the heads. Add the fish and the prawns to the pan and cook slowly for 15 minutes. Taste and adjust the seasoning as necessary. Toss freshly cooked and drained pasta with the sauce in a large frying pan and add a drizzle of olive oil and a little parsley. Serve straight away.

SERVES 4
(as a main, 6 as a starter)

4 tablespoons extra-virgin olive oil,
   plus extra to drizzle
1 shallot, finely chopped
1 carrot, finely chopped
1 celery stalk from the heart with
   some leaves, finely chopped
1 garlic clove, peeled and
   finely chopped
1 bay leaf
a few parsley stalks, finely chopped
5 large raw prawns (shrimp),
   shells and heads on if possible
200 g (7 oz/1 cup) tinned whole
   tomatoes, chopped
pinch of chilli flakes
300 ml (10 fl oz/1¼ cups) prawn stock
   (see page 141) or fish, shellfish or
   vegetable stock, or water
500 g (1 lb 2 oz) mixed flavourful
   white fish such as sea bass,
   sea bream, sole
salt and freshly ground black pepper
320 g (11 oz/3 cups) pasta of your
   choice, to serve
small handful of parsley,
   finely chopped

LINGUINE WITH SEAFOOD

(Linguine ai Frutti di Mare)

SERVES 4

*1 kg (2 lb 3 oz) mixed seafood,
  such as squid rings around 1 cm
  (½ in) thick, clams, queen scallops,
  mussels, raw whole king prawns
  (jumbo shrimp)*
350 g (12 oz) linguine or spaghetti
4 tablespoons extra-virgin olive oil
1 garlic clove, finely chopped
½ red chilli, finely sliced
handful of parsley, roughly chopped
50 ml (2 fl oz/¼ cup) white wine
12 cherry tomatoes, halved
good pinch of salt
30 g (1 oz) Parmesan, finely grated

This delicious dish is best cooked with really fresh shellfish, as the seawater trapped inside the shells is what makes it taste so good. Whole raw king prawns (jumbo shrimp) are also necessary for a great flavour. Most supermarkets tend to sell them already peeled with the heads and tails removed, but the heads contain the most flavour so buy them whole if you can. At the restaurant Gatto Nero on Burano, an island in the Venetian Lagoon, they have a little trick of putting some grated Parmesan in the bottom of the bowl before putting the seafood linguine on top. Usually Italians don't mix cheese and fish but in this case it was really good. They also use more shellfish than pasta. The seafood will cook quickly so prepare everything you need, get the pasta cooking and finish off the sauce.

Clean the shellfish removing the beards from the mussels and drop the clams from a height of around 15 cm (6 in) into a bowl one by one to check for sand – it will come out as they land if dropped from this height. Discard any that are broken or are open and don't close with a tap as they are dead. Remove the tails and shells from the bodies of the prawns leaving their heads on.

Bring a large saucepan of salted water to the boil and cook the pasta until it is only just al dente. Heat the oil in a large frying pan with a lid, add the squid and fry for 2 minutes. Add the rest of the seafood, the garlic, chilli and parsley. Put the lid on the pan and continue to cook for around 4–5 minutes, shaking the pan frequently. When all the shellfish's shells have opened, pour in the wine and let it reduce, uncovered, until the strong smell of alcohol has dissipated. Discard any unopened shellfish. Then add the cherry tomatoes and salt.

Drain the pasta and toss it into the sauce. Let it cook in the juices for a couple of minutes. Divide the Parmesan into the bottom of 4 warm shallow bowls and top with the seafood. the shavings of Pecorino.

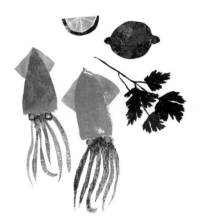

SUNSET AGNOLOTTI STUFFED WITH SEA BASS

(Agnolotti al Tramonto Ripieni di Branzino)

In summer, at our friend Mimmo's wonderful restaurant Osteria Bacchus in Sant'Ambrogio, guests sit opposite on a terrace overlooking the bay of Cefalù. They can enjoy this pasta for dinner, with its vivid colours reflecting the sunset.

Divide the flour between two bowls and crack an egg into each one. Add the tomato purée to one bowl and the saffron water to the other. Follow the instructions for making fresh pasta on page 24. Now take half of each ball of coloured pasta and use your hands or a food processor to blend the two halves together. You will now have three balls of pasta – an orange one, a yellow one and a yellowy-orange one. Cover all three with cling film (plastic wrap) and rest for 20 minutes at room temperature.

   Meanwhile, make the stuffing. Gently fry the onion and garlic in the olive oil until soft. Add the pink peppercorns, lightly crushing them with your fingers as you drop them in. Add the fish to the pan skin-side up to begin with. Cook for 5 minutes, then turn skin-side down and cook for a couple more minutes until tender. Add the lemon juice, zest and salt. Transfer to a large plate. Peel the skin from the fish and discard. Use a fork to mash the flesh to a rough paste. Leave to cool.

   Line up the three balls of pasta in a row and roll them out with a large rolling pin at the same time, dusting them lightly with flour every now and again. Gradually, the three colours will blend together into soft stripes. This can also be done in a pasta machine: divide each ball of pasta into three, then roll each piece into small, walnut-sized balls. You will end up with nine balls. Take three different-coloured balls at a time and roll them together. Feed this into your pasta machine and blended lengths of coloured dough will appear.

   Roll the pasta very thin (around 1 mm thick) and, using a pastry cutter or a large wine glass, cut the pasta into circles around 9 cm (3½ in) across. Put a heaped teaspoon of filling onto the pasta circles and brush a little of the beaten egg around the edge of one half. Fold the circles around the filling and press the edges together to form a half-moon shape. Expel the air from inside as you do this.

SERVES 4
(as a main, 6 as a starter – makes 35 to 40 shapes)

For the pasta
200 g (7 oz/1⅔ cups) '00'
   or very fine semolina flour,
   plus a little extra if necessary
2 eggs (preferably corn-fed
   for colour), plus beaten egg
   to seal the agnolotti
2 tablespoons tomato purée
   (tomato paste)
pinch of saffron powder, mixed
   with 1 teaspoon hot water

For the stuffing
1 onion, finely chopped
1 large garlic clove, peeled
   and finely chopped
2 tablespoons extra-virgin olive oil
2 teaspoons pink peppercorns
3 sea bass or sea bream fillets,
   or any other flavourful white fish
   (approximately 450 g/1 lb)
2 tablespoons lemon juice
finely grated zest of 1 small lemon
salt, to taste

For the sauce
100 g (3½ oz/scant ½ cup)
   salted butter
small handful of sage leaves
few slices red chilli, according
   to taste
3 garlic cloves, skins left on
   and lightly crushed
salt and freshly ground
   black pepper
4 tablespoons fish broth
   or cooking water

Cook the agnolotti in boiling salted water for 4–6 minutes, until al dente. Meanwhile, make the sauce by melting the butter in a large frying pan. Add the sage, chilli and garlic and season. When the agnolotti are done, drain and add to the sauce in the pan with the broth or cooking water. Shake the pan to combine the water and butter. Serve immediately in warmed bowls or plates.

POTATO GNOCCHI

(Patate di Gnocchi)

Bring a large pan of salted water to the boil and cook the potatoes in their skins until tender – this may take up to 1 hour, depending on their size. Drain and peel them while they are still hot, by holding them in one hand with a fork or a cloth and peeling the skin away with a knife in the other hand.

Pass the potatoes through a sieve, ricer or food mill into a large mixing bowl. Stir in the egg with a wooden spoon. Add the salt and a good twist of black pepper, then add half of the flour and combine. Pour the rest of the flour into a mound on to the work surface, make a well in it and put the dough into the well. Use your hands to knead in the rest of the flour to form a firm but pliable dough.

Lightly flour a large board or section of your work surface next to where you are preparing the gnocchi. On a clean surface, roll the dough into long sausages around 2 cm (¾ in) wide. Cut the sausages into 2 cm lengths. Gently roll each piece into a ball between your palms. Use the side of your thumb to carefully roll the ball on a grater to make indentations and form a pattern, then place the gnocco on to your floured board. Repeat this for the rest of the dough. As you roll the gnocchi on the grater a cavity will also from where your thumb was. This and the indentations will be perfect to collect the sauce.

Bring another large saucepan of salted water to the boil. Drop in the gnocchi in two batches and when they bob up to the surface they are done – this takes about 2–4 minutes. Drain well and toss into a sauce heated in a large frying pan.

If you plan to freeze your gnocchi before cooking, spread them out on a well-floured baking tray, making sure they don't touch each other, and put the tray in the freezer. When frozen (which takes around 3 hours), shake off any excess flour and transfer the gnocchi to a freezer bag to take up less space. Use within 3 months. To cook from frozen, allow an extra 1–2 minutes cooking time.

SERVES 8

1 kg (2 lb 3 oz) potatoes
(Desiree work well)
2 eggs, beaten
300 g (10½ oz/2½ cups)
'00' flour
2 teaspoons fine salt
freshly ground black pepper

GNOCCHI

Gnocchi are best made with potatoes that are neither too fluffy nor too waxy and the Italians say they should be boiled in their skins so that the water doesn't saturate the potatoes. The secret to light gnocchi is to trap as much air inside as you can by pushing the cooked potatoes through a sieve, a passatutto (food mill) or a ricer. Freezing gnocchi before they are cooked can give an even better result than cooking from fresh, as they tend to hold their shape better. A Venetian pasta maker told me that his mother would fry any leftover cooked gnocchi for breakfast with butter, and then dust them with sugar and cinnamon.

We visited restaurant Sora Margherita in the Jewish quarter of Rome where the staff were busy making hundreds of potato gnocchi; it was 'gnocchi Giovedì', or 'gnocchi Thursday'. In Rome, many restaurants follow the tradition of serving certain dishes on specific days, and Thursdays are for gnocchi. These gnocchi are perfect served with the oxtail sauce from Coda di Vaccinara on page 114 or with the Sugo Finto on page 75.

POTATO GNOCCHI WITH TOMATO SAUCE, MOZZARELLA & BASIL

(Gnocchi Alla Sorrentina)

SERVES 6

1 quantity Potato Gnocchi
(see page 156)
flour for dusting

To serve
1 quantity of Our Favourite Tomato
Sauce (see page 72)
125 g (4 oz) ball mozzarella
fresh basil leaves

Although this dish originates from Sorrento, its comforting combination of soft potato gnocchi, rich red tomato sauce, moon-white mozzarella and aromatic basil is now served all over the Amalfi Coast. These potato gnocchi are also delicious with ragù or the clam sauce from the 'Ndunderi recipe (see page 147).

Potatoes that are neither too floury nor too waxy are best used to make gnocchi. Gnocchi freeze really well, uncooked. This can sometimes give a lighter result, so consider doubling the quantities and freezing half. To freeze, spread them out on a well-floured tray so that they are not touching. When frozen, shake off excess flour and transfer to freezer bags, seal and freeze. Use within three months. Cook from frozen, allowing 1–2 minutes extra cooking time.

Make the potato gnocchi following the instructions on page 156. Bring a large pan of well-salted water to the boil.

Cook the gnocchi according to page 156. Using a slotted spoon, remove them from the water and toss them into the warm tomato sauce. Serve with the mozzarella torn into pieces and the basil leaves.

PUMPKIN STUFFED GNOCCHI

(Gnocchi Ripieni di Zucca)

Tucked away in the Castello area of Venice we saw an intriguing display of pasta and gnocchi in the window of Pastificio Serenissima. The owner Ivan and he showed us his specialty recipes. He had invented a potato gnocchi that was stuffed with pumpkin and cheese. Pumpkins are available all year round in the Veneto. The two main types are the smooth green *zucca mantovana*, which has bright orange flesh and is always available, and the seasonal *zucca barucca* with a knobbly, bumpy skin. Ivan told us to adjust the quantity of bread according to how much water there is in the pumpkin.

Preheat the oven to 180°C (350°F/Gas 4). Put the pumpkin in a large baking tin, cover with foil and roast for 40 minutes. Remove the foil and roast for another 15 minutes or until soft. Make sure the pumpkin doesn't brown. Remove from the oven and allow to cool. Put the flesh into a food processor and blend or into a large mixing bowl and mash by hand. Add the rest of filling ingredients, stir to combine and set aside.

Make the potato gnocchi following the instructions on page 156. Instead of making sausage shapes roll out the dough with a rolling pin into a rough rectangle 5 mm (¼ in) thick. Fill a piping bag with the filling mixture and 4 cm (1½ in) down from the top edge pipe a 2 cm (¾ in) thick sausage of stuffing. Fold the top edge of the dough over the filling and seal it in by gently pressing down with your fingers. Cut the length of gnocchi away from the rectangle and cut into pieces around 2 cm (¾ in) wide and 4 cm (1½ in) long. Set aside on a clean tea towel (dishcloth). Repeat the piping, folding, sealing and cutting process down the rest of the rectangle.

Melt the butter with the sage leaves and black pepper in a large frying pan over a low heat. Bring a large saucepan of salted water to a gentle boil. Drop in the gnocchi and when they float up to the surface they are done – this takes about 2 minutes.

Remove the gnocchi from the water with a slotted spoon and add them into the frying pan. Toss through and serve in warm bowls with Parmesan.

SERVES 6
(as a main, 8 as a starter – makes 90–100 gnocchi)

1 quantity Potato Gnocchi
  (see page 156)
flour for dusting

For the filling
300 g (10½ oz) peeled,
  seeded pumpkin, cut into
  approximately 5 cm (2 in) cubes
100 g (3½ oz) Parmesan,
  finely grated
1 egg, plus 1 egg yolk
150 g (5 oz/2 cups) soft
  breadcrumbs
grating of nutmeg
1 teaspoon salt
1 sprig of rosemary,
  finely chopped

For the sauce
100 g (3½ oz/scant ½ cup)
  salted butter
15–20 sage leaves
freshly ground black pepper
50 g (2 oz) Parmesan,
  finely grated

PUMPKIN GNOCCHI FOR LAMB RAGÙ WITH SPICES

(Maccheroni di Zucca con Ragù di Agnello Speziato)

SERVES 6–8

1.6 kg (3 lb 8 oz) butternut
  squash, approximately
  2 squashes
3 tablespoons extra-virgin olive oil
3 eggs plus 2 egg yolks
100 g (3½ oz) Parmesan,
  grated
300 g (10½ oz/2½ cups)
  '00' flour
salt and freshly ground
  black pepper
sunflower oil

These were originally called *maccheroni* in the Veneto during the medieval period. They have continued to be made to this day, usually with the green fat pumpkins called *mantovana*. Mario, the chef at Bistrot de Venise, showed us a way to make these pumpkin gnocchi by pushing the mixture through a piping bag and snipping off pieces into boiling water with scissors. He serves them with the equally ancient recipe for Lamb Ragù with Spices (see page 111). We've used readily-available butternut squash instead of *mantovana*.

Preheat the oven to 180°C (350°F/Gas 4). Wash the butternut squash and cut into wedges around 5 cm (2 in) at the thickest part leaving the skin on. Put the wedges into a baking tray and brush over with the olive oil. Cook for 30–40 minutes until soft. Remove from the oven and leave to cool. Scoop the flesh off the skins into a food processor. Add the eggs, egg yolks, cheese, flour and seasoning, and blend until smooth.

Bring a large saucepan of well-salted water to the boil. Put the gnocchi mixture into a piping bag with a 2 cm (¾ in) nozzle. Over the pan of boiling water, push the mixture through the bag and snip off the first gnocchi at 2 cm so that it falls into the water. Work fast and continue until a third of the mixture is used. When the gnocchi come to the surface they are cooked. Scoop them out with a slotted spoon and put into a warm serving dish coated with some sunflower oil. Brush more oil over the gnocchi in the dish so they don't stick together. Repeat with the rest of the mixture in 2 more batches, each time coat the gnocchi in the dish with some sunflower oil. The gnocchi can be kept in the fridge or frozen like this, or used straight away. To serve with ragù (see page 111), heat the ragù in a large non-stick frying pan and then add the gnocchi. If the gnocchi have been stored in the fridge reheat them by putting them in boiling salted water for 30 seconds, drain and add to the ragù.

CHESTNUT & POTATO GNOCCHI

(Gnocchi di Castagne e Patate)

SERVES 4

500 g (1 lb 2 oz) fluffy potatoes,
   such as Desiree or King Edward,
   unpeeled
75 g (2½ oz/scant ⅔ cup) chestnut
   or '00' flour
1 teaspoon fine salt, plus extra
   for the cooking water
freshly ground black pepper,
   to taste
1 egg, plus 1 egg yolk, beaten

Chestnut flour is naturally sweet and therefore the gnocchi lend themselves to a hearty meat ragù such as the one on page 99, or a simple sauce such as butter and sage sauce.

Make the potato gnocchi following the instructions on page 156. Bring a large pan of well-salted water to the boil.

Cook the gnocchi according to page 156. Using a slotted spoon, and toss them into the tomato sauce.

If you plan to freeze your gnocchi before cooking, spread them out on a well-floured baking tray, making sure they don't touch each other, and put the tray in the freezer. When frozen, shake off any excess flour and transfer the gnocchi to a freezer bag to take up less space. Use within 3 months. To cook from frozen, allow an extra 1–2 minutes cooking time.

SMOKED CHEESE GNOCCHI

(Gnocchi Ripieni)

I absolutely love these light little dumplings of smoked cheese and ricotta, which are usually served with a simple tomato sauce. The centre melts, giving the appearance that the gnocchi are stuffed with melted cheese. They are completely different to potato gnocchi.

First prepare your chosen tomato sauce.

Next, mix all the gnocchi ingredients except the semolina together in a bowl, using an electric whisk to achieve a smooth mixture. Bring a large pan of well-salted water to the boil.

If making large gnocchi, use tablespoons; if making small gnocchi, use teaspoons. To shape the gnocchi, use 2 spoons to make quenelles: take a spoonful of the mixture, hold a spoon in each hand and form ovals like small rugby balls by scraping the mixture from one spoon to the other, squeezing it together as you work. Roll the shapes into the semolina to coat them, then drop them in batches into the boiling water. They will float to the surface when cooked. Lift them out gently using a slotted spoon and add them directly to the pan containing the sauce of your choice. Make sure the sauce is warm and gently toss the gnocchi in the sauce to coat. Serve immediately with basil leaves and shavings of Parmesan or Grana Padano.

SERVES 4
(makes 12 large or 20 small gnocchi)

*1 quantity of tomato sauce
of your choice*

For the gnocchi
*250 g (9 oz) ricotta drained
1 egg
35 g (1¼ oz/¼ cup) '00'
  or plain flour
50 g (2 oz) Parmesan,
  finely grated
25 g (1 oz) smoked cheese,
  such as scamorza or smoked
  Cheddar, finely grated
salt and freshly ground
  black pepper
50 g (2 oz/⅓ cup) semolina
  to serve
basil leaves
Parmesan or Grana Padano
  shavings*

SEMOLINA GNOCCHI

(Gnocchi Alla Romana)

SERVES 6

150 g (5 oz) salted butter
1 litre (34 fl oz) milk
1 teaspoon salt
250 g (9 oz/2 cups) fine
   semolina, sieved
100 g (3½ oz) Parmesan,
   finely grated
2 egg yolks, beaten

This is a particularly Roman way of making gnocchi without a potato in sight. It is a rediscovery in our house since writing the recipe for this book. I have to say I thought it was going to be heavy and rather dismissed it. Giancarlo and the boys loved it, but when we made it for the book photoshoot it was the girls in our crew who succumbed to the dark side. Now I am a convert and very happy to spread the word about the warm, crispy, cheesy delights of semolina gnocchi.

Heat the oven to 180°C (350°F/Gas 6). Butter a baking tray measuring around 40 x 30 cm (16 x 12 in) and at least 2 cm (¾ in) deep and have it ready at your side – you will need to pour the semolina into it quickly before it starts to set. In a large saucepan, bring the milk to the boil with the salt, then slowly sprinkle in the sieved semolina stirring constantly with a whisk. When it starts to thicken remove the pan from the heat. Keep whisking the semolina off the heat to stop it becoming lumpy; add 100 g (3½ oz) of the butter and whisk until fully incorporated. Add half of the Parmesan, both the beaten egg yolks and whisk again. Remember to work quickly as you don't want it to set in the pan. Pour into the buttered oven tray. Put a layer of baking parchment over the top of the semolina and smooth it down into a flat layer around 2 cm (¾ in) deep. Leave to cool and set. It will take around 1 hour in a cool room.

Meanwhile, generously butter an oven dish measuring around 20 x 30 cm (8 x 12 in) big. When the semolina has cooled and set firm use a 6 cm (2½ in) cutter (or wine glass) to cut out circles. The trimmings can be compacted together and cut out too so nothing is wasted. Lay the circles into the buttered dish and top with flecks of the remaining butter. Scatter over the rest of the cheese. Cook in the oven for around 20 minutes until browned and bubbling hot. Serve on its own.

THANK YOU

A great big thank you:

To Kate Pollard, publisher, and
Kajal Mistry, commissioning editor,
for the great idea of making a pasta
book. We have loved collating our
favourite recipes our travels in Italy.

To Molly Ahuja, senior editor, for
overseeing the whole book and her
endless patience with my corrections.

To Helen Cathcart for the stunning
photography, I never tire of seeing
the photographs which are now
very happy memories of time spent
together in Italy and the UK.

To Designer Claire Warner for the
bright, happy and gorgeous design.

To Illustrator Jill Calder for the
great cover and little illustrations
which add that final touch to
a beautiful book.

ABOUT THE AUTHORS

Owners of London's Caffè Caldesi, Caldesi in Campagna in Bray, and the Marylebone La Cucina Caldesi cooking school, Katie and Giancarlo Caldesi have a passion for Italian food. They have spent over 16 years teaching students at every level, and have written 11 cookbooks. Katie and Giancarlo have two children, Giorgio and Flavio.

caldesi.com

INDEX

The Long and the Short of Pasta
by Katie & Giancarlo Caldesi

First published in 2018
by Hardie Grant Books, an imprint
of Hardie Grant Publishing

Hardie Grant Books (London)
52–54 Southwark Street
London SE1 1UN

Hardie Grant Books (Melbourne)
Building 1, 658 Church Street
Richmond, Victoria 3121

hardiegrantbooks.com

British Library Cataloguing-in-Publication
Data. A catalogue record for this book
is available from the British Library.

ISBN: 978-1-78488-169-6

Publisher: Kate Pollard
Commissioning Editor: Kajal Mistry
Senior Editor: Molly Ahuja
Publishing Assistant: Eila Purvis
Design: Claire Warner Studio
Illustrator © Jill Calder
Icons on page 19 created by Daniela Baptista,
James Mayle, Alex Muravev, Hea Poh Lin,
Ismael Ruiz, Dara Ullrich and Andrey Vasiliev
from the Noun Project
Photography © Helen Cathcart
Indexer: Cathy Heath
Colour Reproduction by p2d
Printed and bound in China by Leo Paper Group

Recipes in this book were first published
in The Amalfi Coast, Venice, Rome, Sicily
and Tuscany